Performance
in the
Museum

Performance in the Museum

Pierre Saurisse

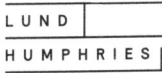

LUND
HUMPHRIES

First published in 2025 by Lund Humphries

Lund Humphries
Second Home Spitalfields
68-80 Hanbury Street
London E1 5JL
UK

www.lundhumphries.com
info@lundhumphries.com

Performance in the Museum

ISBN   978-1-84822-380-6
eBook (Mobi)   978-1-84822-383-7
eBook (ePub)   978-1-84822-382-0
eBook (PDF)   978-1-84822-381-3

A Cataloguing-in-Publication record for this
book is available from the British Library

Copy edited by Michela Parkin
Designed by Wolfe Hall
Set in Mediaan by Dávid Molnár
and WH Aldine Mono by Wolfe Hall
Printed by Tallinna Raamatutrükikoda, Estonia

Lund Humphries' EU GPSR Authorised Representative
is LOGOS EUROPE, 9 rue Nicolas Poussin, 17000,
LA ROCHELLE, France
contact@logoseurope.eu

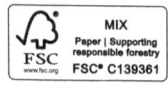

NEW DIRECTIONS IN CONTEMPORARY ART

Series Editor: Marcus Verhagen, Senior Lecturer, Sotheby's Institute of Art, London

A series of newly commissioned, engaging, critical texts identifying key topics and trends in contemporary art practice and discussing their impact on the wider art world and beyond. The art world is changing rapidly as artists avail themselves of new technologies, travel ever more widely, reach out to new audiences and tackle urgent issues, from climate change to mass migration. The purpose of the series is to discuss these and other changes, in texts that are accessible, stimulating and polemical.

INTERNATIONAL SERIES ADVISORY BOARD

Foreword

In the summer and autumn of 2008, sprinters could be seen running the length of Tate Britain's Duveen Galleries at 30-second intervals. Instructed to run at full pelt, 'as if their lives depended on it', they were executing Martin Creed's *Work No. 850*.[1] Projects annually commissioned for the space, which is 300 feet long, have generally taken the form of monumental sculpture: a replica of a house, a pair of decommissioned fighter planes, an army of life-size figures. Creed's decision to create a performance piece was a novel departure, but it was also a response to the site: 'I wanted to use the whole space', he said at the time, 'instead of putting an object in it. The runner is like a guide showing you the whole space.'[2] But the work was not just an effort to reveal 'the whole space'. It was a teasing and disruptive commentary on both the Duveen Galleries and the institution of the art museum. By turning the halls into a running track, he drew out the vast proportions and pomp of the neo-classical design while poking fun at the assumption that the museum is a setting for slow and elevating contemplation.

For a long time it was thought that performance and the museum were not natural bedfellows. The first was shown primarily in alternative and public spaces, far from the more hidebound institutions of the cultural establishment. And the second focused on the display and conservation of objects, not the hosting of events. Creed expertly played on these tensions.

But museums have come under growing pressure to show performance. They have accommodated it with a view to drawing in new audiences and recognising and profiting from the immense popularity of artists such as Yoko Ono and Marina Abramović. Above all, they have exhibited performance in order to give a fuller and more vital account of the art of the recent past. Pierre Saurisse's book tells the story of that process of incorporation. With learning and insight, he traces the history of performance in the museum, highlighting changes in artistic practice on the one hand and new protocols of acquisition, documentation and display on the other. Too often these histories have been traced separately. By weaving them together, Saurisse significantly enhances our understanding of both.

Marcus Verhagen

Performance and the Missions of the Museum

In 1963, in the courtyard adjacent to her studio in Paris, Marta Minujín set on fire her own sculptures with a torch after they had been covered with cream, painted silver and smashed with an axe by friends (fig.1). Minujín herself was wrapped in a piece of white cloth by Christo, dozens of birds were released and rabbits set free to roam. The action marked a shift in her practice towards action and ephemerality. Positioning herself in a particular segment of the art system that resists commercialisation and institutionalisation, the artist declared, 'I felt and believed that art was something more important for human beings than the eternity that only a few cultured ones would attain in museums and galleries'.[1]

A joyous cataclysm, Minujín's *La destrucción* (The Destruction) claimed the spirit of the underground and gave mainstream art the cold shoulder. Having works smashed and charred stands precisely in opposition to the museum's mission to safeguard art. Her messy, unruly and volatile course of actions, which ended up with the arrival of firemen, was also ostensibly unadaptable to the logistics and regulations of an institutional setting. In its wreckful energy it echoed Jean Tinguely's enormous sculpture *Homage to New York*, which destroyed itself with the help of the artist in the garden of the Museum of Modern Art in New York in 1960, a work that Dore Ashton saw as an 'art of destructions enacted – not concealed and held captive as they are in "ordinary" painting'.[2]

The impracticality of art based on human presence in the context of the museum punctuates the history of performance.

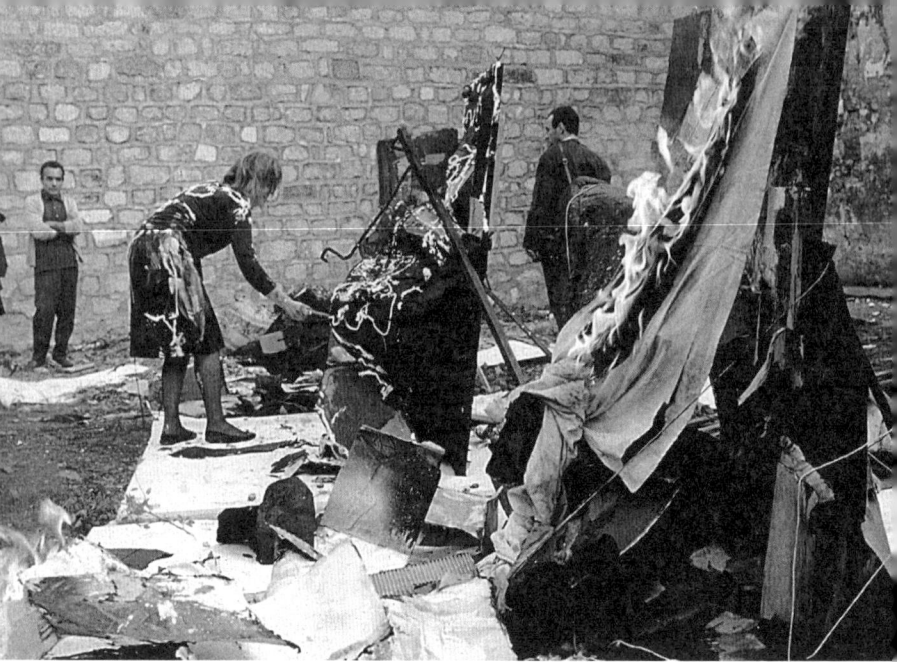

Fig.1   Marta Minujín, *La destrucción* [The Destruction], Paris, 1963

Neither is it evidently suited to galleries designed for objects,
nor to the temporal structure of exhibitions running over weeks
or months. Moreover, the advent of performance has often
taken by surprise museum staff without specific professional
training or experience and left curators, museum directors,
conservators and registrars unprepared. Meanwhile, and despite
this, performance has put a foot in the door of the institution
and threaded its way to the museum.

   A generation later, a measure of how far performance
had come since its early days was given when artists
who had thrived in the underground were honoured in large
exhibitions, past performances long known through a handful
of grainy black-and-white photographs were restaged,
or new performance material was excavated and brought
into collections. While the surge of interest in performance
has permeated the contemporary art scene at large, notably
biennials and art fairs, the museum occupies the unique
position of being a public place meant to be open to all,

endowed with a civic duty and accountable to its citizens. A place where reputations are made and whose activities are followed by a broad audience, its approach to performance is particularly noted.

The integration of performance into the repository for objects that is the museum has not happened organically, but in fits and starts. The diverse challenges posed by live works did not appear all at once; they were identified and addressed with unequal intensity over time as performance emerged, later became the object of historical scrutiny and then entered collections. This book explores this phenomenon through three essential missions of the museum, namely presentation, conservation and acquisition. To reflect the various degrees of urgency felt by the museum at different times as it has responded to performance, each chapter is devoted to one of those missions in a specific period. These periods are turning points, moments of crisis, bouts of experimentation and bursts of activity during which the problems of the display, the afterlife or the acquisition of a performance work were experienced with particular acuity. The aim of this book is to identify and investigate portions of time when questions posed to the museum by performance, and to performance by the museum, made a significant advance.

The first chapter focuses on the presentation of performance in the 1960s and 1970s. From the outset, it was shown in commercial galleries, often on the occasion of exhibition openings, placed at the centre of festivals organised by artists and courted by museums keen to accommodate the sharpest edges of contemporary art. At the same time, performance's self-consciousness in creating a position for itself within the art world has also translated into the questioning of its relationship to the museum. While the institution represents the prospect of recognition for the art form, it is also seen as a figure of authority whose rejection can assert a powerful political stance. These tensions are played out as the model of the exhibition, and its object-focused conventions and modes of display, is called into question by live works.

The next chapter starts at a moment when it became apparent that early performance was becoming history, bringing the question of its conservation to the fore. Intrinsically ephemeral, performance seems antithetical to the purpose of prolonging the longevity of artworks. In the 1990s large and ambitious exhibitions were mounted in museums which set out to address the history of performance. Confronted with the absence of the works themselves, the afterlife of performance was addressed through the lens of the object, notably reconstructions. Then, around 2000, a shift privileged live action in the form of re-enactments. This period resulted in a new awareness of the role played by documentation.

Chapter Three examines how performance entered museum collections in the 2000s. In terms of the number of works, the development of performance-related collections was largely dominated by videos, photographs and objects. In terms of radicality, the acquisition of live works has brought about pervasive changes in the possibilities of enriching collections. The emergence of this phenomenon is examined in this chapter through acquisition procedures themselves, describing what is actually acquired when a live work enters a museum collection. In both types of acquisition, material and immaterial, the museum may be engaged in a process of formalisation which manifests itself in the characterisation of a live performance or the creation of ensembles of objects.

The presentation, conservation and acquisition of performance works are examined together in the last chapter, which spans the period from 2010 onwards. As performance has become increasingly visible in the contemporary art scene, the museum has engaged in intense research to confront issues arising as a result. Discussion has tended to be directed at the institution itself, its role and its mission vis à vis performance. The institutional embrace of performance, the modes of inclusion of live works in exhibitions and the role of dance in this process, and the practicalities of the conservation and acquisition of performance are among questions which sparked discussions and were the focus of research programmes. For the museum, it has been a period of deep introspection.

Although this book covers the period from the emergence of performance up to the present, it does not adopt an encyclopaedic perspective, and it takes an unsystematic approach within a broadly chronological framework. The focus on key moments of specific missions of the museum leaves out many aspects of the history of performance. It is a fragmentary history in that it privileges the role played by the museum, mostly museums as such but also establishments without a collection, generally setting aside other venues such as artist-run galleries, private homes or studios. None of these places are 'neutral' of course, and any artwork is inevitably seen against the background of its setting, and framed by it. The museum, beyond its function as a physical container, is regarded as an institution of particular significance for its role in considering art from the points of view of its display, conservation and collection, with its teams of professionals and experts, its architecture, its resources and limitations, its rules and regulations. Performance has evolved in part against the museum and in part with and inside it, one could almost say through it.

What is understood by performance throughout its history has also changed. An umbrella term aggregating works which could be labelled, elsewhere, 'happening', 'action' or 'event', it includes a wide spectrum of practices. The museum has profusely used the elasticity of the notion of performance, for example in exhibitions moving around this art form from the orbit of the object, or in the classification and distribution of acquisitions in various departments. Although based on live presence, the word performance is also used about works consisting of traces of actions, rather than the action itself. In 1998 Amelia Jones attempted to clarify the situation by using the term 'Body Art' in reference to works 'that take place through an enactment of the artist's body, whether it be in a "performance" setting or in the relative privacy of the studio, that is then documented such that it can be experienced subsequently through photography, film, video, and / or text'.[3] The relation between action and its traces has been central to the behaviour of the museum towards performance, and live works are considered here along with their material side, be it preparatory sketches, props, sets, documentation, photographs, videos or works made after the event. While the taxonomy distinguishing live action from performance-related material tends to fade, live action still stands out as a specific challenge to the routine of museums, whose modes of operation are historically rooted in the object.

Chapter 1

Presentation: Staging Performance in the Museum, 1960s–1970s

Performance appeared in an art scene defined by the object. It affirmed its legitimacy and very existence in an institutional context not suited to a form of art which was ephemeral, unfixed and comprised living beings. It was, above all, logistically unfit for the museum. Looking at the roots of performance as far back as the early 20th century, when artists engaged in painting, music, literature or theatre 'needed public platforms beyond the limited worlds of those disciplines',[1] it began in venues such as cafes, among them Cabaret Voltaire in Zürich. After the Second World War it gained significant exposure in places as diverse as a department store (Allan Kaprow, *Bon Marché*, 1963) or a slaughterhouse (Wolf Vostell, *In Ulm, um Ulm und um Ulm herum* (In Ulm, near Ulm, around Ulm, 1964). It was not, however, absent from the art gallery, notably finding its place in exhibition openings. Meanwhile, festivals organised by artists themselves played a crucial role in consolidating the sense of an off-centre community.

The relationship between performance and the art institution is characterised neither by a full embrace nor by outright rejection. It is formed of contradictions, mutual attraction and scepticism. In Japan, for example, the group Gutai broke the mould of art-making early on by showing not only paintings and sculptures but also live works, and when its first exhibition opened in 1955 in Ohara Hall in Tokyo, with Kazuo Shiraga wrestling in a pool of mud (*Challenging Mud*, 1955) and Saburo Murakami bursting through large screens of paper

(*Six Holes*, 1955), it was strategically scheduled to coincide with important juried exhibitions taking place in the city. This timing, aligning eccentric and burgeoning forms of art with the traditional artistic calendar of the location, was repeated in the second Gutai exhibition a year later.

Positioning performance in relation to the museum, and the perspectives of recognition it represents, proved key for the new art form to carve out its place in the art scene. In the context of social and political upheavals and cultural rebellion in the 1960s, performance sought to establish its legitimacy while thriving on the independence it enjoyed outside institutional structures. The ties between performance and the big machinery of the museum are marked by this dichotomy. In the exhibition, in particular, this is played out as the requirement of the museum to adapt flexibly to performance and the capacity of performance to preserve its integrity within the institutional setting.

THE CURATORIAL CONUNDRUM

The Commercial Gallery as a Stage

The first artists who contributed to the emergence of performance were primarily engaged in the production of paintings or sculptures. Performance secured a foothold in the gallery by means of material works, especially by conflating the site of production of art with that of its display. A precedent was set by Georges Mathieu when in 1952 he was photographed making large paintings at the Studio Paul Facchetti in Paris, where his exhibition was to be held. While borrowing the paradigm of Jackson Pollock painting before the photographer Hans Namuth in his studio in 1950, the French artist moved the act of creation from the studio to the exhibition space. This migration of the creative process to the gallery gained traction as making a painting became more spectacular, in the literal sense that it was interesting to watch. Very conscious of the visual attraction of himself at work, Mathieu wore a Middle Ages-inspired cloth helmet and strips of fabric around his calves as he painted *La Bataille de Bouvines* (The Battle of Bouvines) for the camera in 1954.

The gallery was a stage for the artist at work when Yves Klein instructed female models to cover their naked bodies with blue pigment and press themselves against a canvas at the Galerie Internationale d'art contemporain in Paris in 1960, and when Niki de Saint Phalle finished off paintings by shooting at them with a rifle at the opening of her show at Galerie J, also in Paris, in 1961. In the same spirit, Piero Manzoni wrote his name on a dozen people at the opening of the exhibition *Castellani & Manzoni* at Galleria La Tartaruga in Rome in 1961, where his *Achromes* and other works made with cotton and wool were on display.

Performance often intruded into the gallery through the very social event that is the exhibition opening. For artists, it was vital that the procedural part of their practice became visible, and for galleries, hosting live events gave them an adventurous and experimental edge. For both, live events had the advantage of attracting attention and generating publicity. In 1961 the opening of the group Zero's exhibition at Galerie Schmela in Düsseldorf was noticed for *ZERO: Edition, Exposition, Demonstration*, an action involving performers dressed in black cardboard outfits marked with white zeros (fig.2). After they painted a large 'zero' on the paving stones in front of the gallery, a huge balloon was released into the air. The event, which was attended by a large crowd, was filmed and broadcast on German television the next day.

Whether or not scheduled to mark the openings of shows, performance sprang up, in large part, grafted onto gallery exhibitions. This placed it in physical proximity, if not in dialogue, with material works. When Atsuko Tanaka displayed herself wearing the entanglement of lightbulbs and wires that is *Electric Dress* (1956) in an exhibition in Tokyo in 1956, she technically presented a performance while also serving as a support for her soft sculpture. She carved out a place for her still performance in the exhibition by creating a relationship between mediums as she stood in front of drawings and

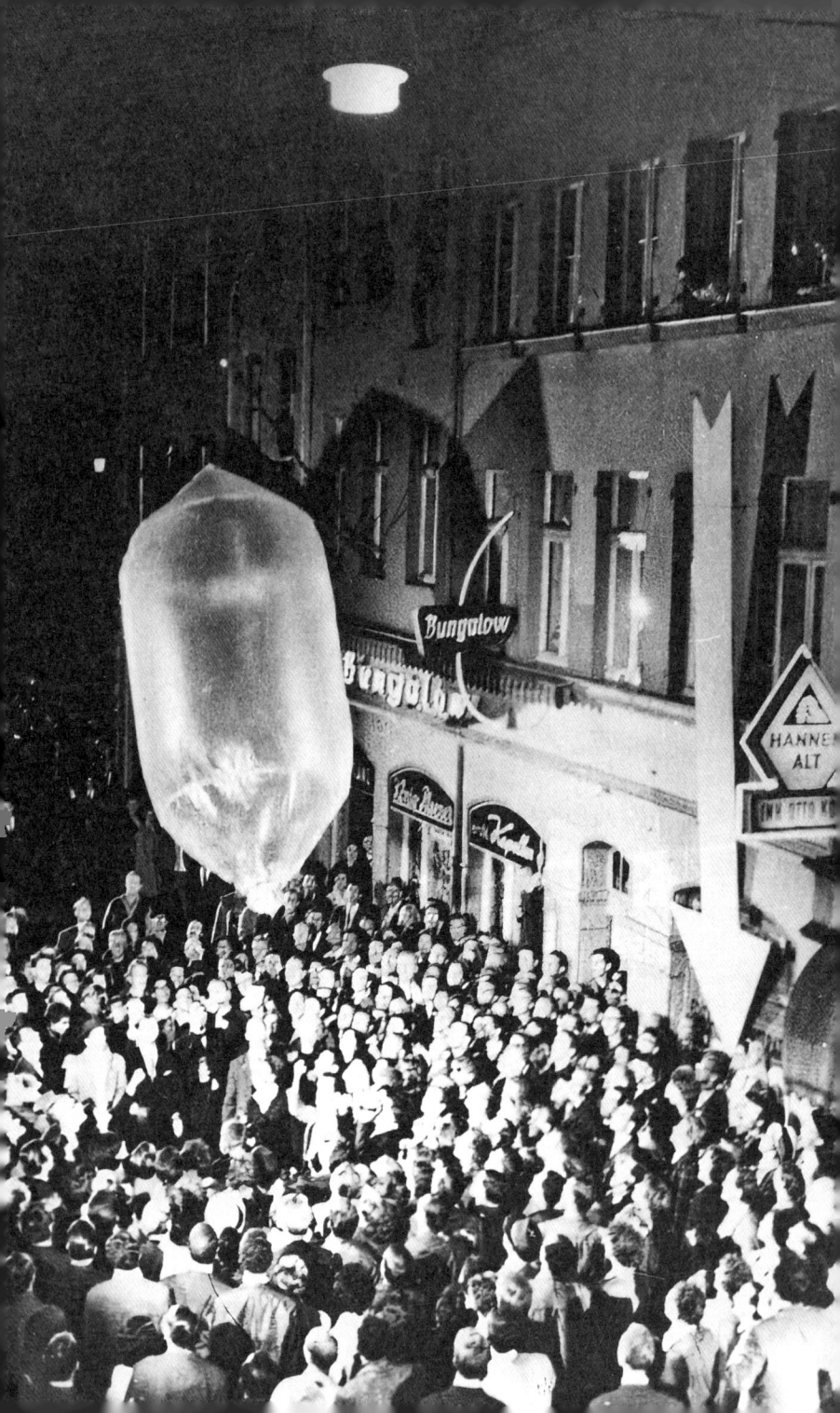

paintings made for the preparation of the 'dress'. In Paris Tetsumi Kudo made his name by executing the performance *Philosophy of Impotence* in two group exhibitions curated by the artist Jean-Jacques Lebel in 1962 (at Galerie Raymond Cordier and in a rented film studio). Then at the 1963 Paris biennial at the Musée d'art moderne de la Ville de Paris, Kudo, dressed in a kimono and equipped with a sword, presented among his sculptures *Hara-Kiri of Humanism*, mimicking the ritual of *hara-kiri*, and immediately afterwards *Bottled Humanism*, in which he squeezed dolls into glass jars before throwing them to the audience standing nearby.

From the early 1960s, some galleries stood out for showing live works in exhibitions, a fact occurring to a significant degree in Europe. Galerie Raymond Cordier in Paris opened the group show *Pour conjurer l'esprit de catastrophe* (To Conjure up the Spirit of Catastrophe) with Lebel's eponymous performance in 1962, Galerie Schmela in Düsseldorf hosted Joseph Beuys's *How to Explain Pictures to a Dead Hare* at the opening of his exhibition of sculptures and drawings in 1965, and the same year Wolf Vostell executed *Phänomene* at Galerie René Block in Berlin during his exhibition *Wolf Vostell: "Phänomene", Verwischungen, Partituren* ("Phenomenons", Blur, Scores). As for Günter Brus, in 1965 he walked the streets of Vienna dressed in a suit and entirely painted white, a thick black line dividing his body from head to toe (*Wiener Spaziergang* [Vienna Walk]); this performance was strategically scheduled the day before the opening of his exhibition at Galerie Junge Generation in the same city.

The Festival: A Dynamic Exhibition

As performance started to be hosted in commercial galleries well versed in experimentation, it also found a haven in artist-run galleries. This phenomenon was particularly notable in New York, and Allan Kaprow was instrumental in this evolution. In 1959 he became involved in the programme

Fig.2 *ZERO: Edition, Exposition, Demonstration,* performance in front of Galerie Schmela, Düsseldorf, 1961

of the Reuben Gallery, a commercial venture modelled
on alternative spaces where, as Lawrence Alloway wrote,
'There was ... an easy contact between artist and gallery,
an affinity between the act of production and the act of
presentation, which was very different from the regular
marketing of promotional activities of art dealers'.[2] The Reuben
Gallery was inaugurated in 1959 with Kaprow's *18 Happenings
in 6 Parts* – from which the word 'Happening' originates –
which was executed in a temporary environment made of sheets
of plastic, mirrors and painted light bulbs, among other objects.
Presented most evenings over a week, *18 Happenings in 6 Parts*
established a model for the presentation of performances over
a certain period of time, rather than as one-offs. This model
was followed by Claes Oldenburg in *Ray Gun Spex* in 1960,
a three-day festival of performances by artists such as Jim
Dine, Al Hansen, Dick Higgins and Kaprow which took place
at the Judson Gallery, a favoured home for performances
and ephemeral installations housed in the Judson Memorial
Church in New York.

The festival soon came to be regarded as a mode of
presentation particularly suited to performance. The term,
usually used in the context of events dedicated to music, theatre
or cinema, found particular credence with Fluxus, a group
versed in the conceptual side of performance and whose artists
had often performed together in theatres, but also in galleries,
private homes and on the street. With Fluxus, 'festival' denoted
a series of performances (or 'events', as they were often called)
taking place over a certain period, for example the *Fluxus
Internationale Festspiele Neuester Musik* (International Fluxus
Festival of New Music), held in a municipal auditorium
in Wiesbaden in 1962.

In the realm of the visual arts, the notion of festival gained
currency as a non-static exhibition, where things are not simply
put on display but happen. The art critic Pierre Restany, eager
to emphasise the engagement of his stable of artists with action
and process, organised in 1961 the *Festival du Nouveau Réalisme*
(Festival of New Realism) at Galerie Muratore in Nice during

which Arman destroyed an antique-style piece of furniture. Loosely associated with this group of 'New Realists', Daniel Spoerri put on in London, in 1962, what he called a *Festival of Misfits*, even though it was, essentially, an exhibition. This exhibition, however, escaped inertia as it included works in motion, works inviting audience participation (Emmett Williams's *Universal Poem*, for example), as well as a performance by Ben Vautier, who made the gallery his temporary home and lived there, visible from the street through the window, for the duration of the exhibition. In 1963, in Vienna, the Viennese Actionists held a *Festival of Psycho-Physical Naturalism* in a private basement space (the series of performances was interrupted by the police). Inherently a dynamic formation, the festival constituted a salutary counter-model to art exhibitions and their sense of stationary display.

Festivals were also essential in asserting the idea that artists themselves could assume the responsibility for calibrating the presentation of performance. By pushing live action to the foreground, festivals were crucial in achieving a confluence of ideas and consolidating a sense of community among the pioneers of the new art form. A key role was played by Jean-Jacques Lebel's *Festivals de la libre expression* (Festivals of Free Expression), whose first edition, at the American Center in Paris in 1964, included performances by Tetsumi Kudo, Carolee Schneemann, Ben Vautier and Lebel himself. Another groundbreaking event was the *Destruction in Art Symposium*, a festival (and also a symposium) masterminded by Gustav Metzger in 1966. The event, held at the Africa House in London, included performances by Günter Brus, Otto Muehl, Yoko Ono, Ralph Ortiz and Wolf Vostell among other artists. By leading the presentation of performance, artists framed the context of its emergence in their own terms. As Metzger explained, with the *Destruction in Art Symposium* '[we] didn't want to connect to anything in the establishment world, nor did we want to align with the underground'.[3] Such a position stood for a significant section of performance at the time as it claimed its place within the art world, but often towards the edge of it.

Jenevive Nykolak has pointed to the important role played
by works in motion in bringing time-based art into museums.
For Pontus Hultén for example, who was appointed Director
of the Moderna Museet in Stockholm in 1959, 'kinetic art served
as a direct impetus for the introduction of live, durational
forms', Nykolak writes. She explains, 'Hultén transposed
his early enthusiasm for kinetic art into his democratizing
reconfiguration of the museum as a dynamic, multidisciplinary
zone, garnering the Swedish museum an international
reputation and culminating in his leadership role at the
Centre Georges Pompidou in Paris in 1977'.[4] Sculptures
and installations endowed with motion or involving audience
participation, as well as performance, assume unfixed or
uncontainable configurations, and they deeply destabilised
display and spectatorship conventions. At the Moderna Museet
in 1961, the exhibition *Rörelse i konsten* (Movement in Art)
featured Allan Kaprow's *Stockroom* (1961), a large installation
(not included in the original version of the show earlier that
year at the Stedelijk Museum in Amsterdam under the title
Bewogen Beweging [Moving Movement]) which comprised a set
of cardboard boxes that could be painted, sprayed, moved and
hung by the visitors. Billy Klüver, an engineer who collaborated
on artist projects, recalled, 'When I looked through the door,
not one cardboard box was left hanging. In less than an hour,
the people had torn down the cardboard boxes, splashed paint
on them, kicked them and stamped on them. The room was
a total ruin.'[5]

Under the bold and ambitious directorship of Hultén,
the Moderna Museet organised in 1964 a programme of stand-
alone performances, much like a festival, with *5 New York
Evenings*. The series of events included Robert Rauschenberg's
Elgin Tie (1964), in which the artist slid down a rope hanging
from the ceiling and ended in a barrel of water while a cow
wandered past (a reference to the Elgin Marbles and its representation of men and animals), as well as works by dancers

such as Steve Paxton. Dance was also a way of opening
a breach in the fixity of gallery displays and asserting the
museum's experimental agenda. After the Merce Cunningham
Dance Company's dance show *Museum Event* was presented
at Museum des 20. Jahrhunderts (Museum of the 20th Century)
in Vienna in 1964, other such 'museum events' were hosted in
the following years by various art institutions, most of which,
Nykolak has noted, had opened recently.

Perhaps unparalleled in its support for performance was
the Instituto Torcuato Di Tella in Buenos Aires. The most
influential contemporary art institution in the city, this
privately run art centre was the best window for the thriving
performance scene in Latin America. Under military rule and
amid widespread censorship, the Di Tella, as it was known,
played an important role in placing performance on the
international art map. The year 1966 marked the peak of its
performance activities, as it hosted the Argentinian instalment
of *Three Countries Happening*, performed by Marta Minujín
in Buenos Aires, Allan Kaprow in New York and Wolf Vostell
in Berlin, the three artists simultaneously executing instructions
sent between them by telegram and telephone.

The Di Tella was instrumental in broadening the audience
for performance. In 1967, 500 people attended Oscar Masotta's
Sobre Happenings (About Happenings), in which several artists,
among them Masotta himself, amalgamated fragments of
performances by Michael Kirby, Claes Oldenburg and Carolee
Schneemann. At the Di Tella, Masotta also conceived *Para
inducir el espíritu de la imagen* (To Induce the Spirit of the
Image, 1966), in which a brightly lit row of people just stood
in front of the audience, and in the same period he worked
on a festival of performances which, had the project not fallen
through, would have involved the Museo de Arte Moderno
de Buenos Aires. Masotta explained, 'By acting this way – i.e.,
by planning out Happenings within an official framework: the
presence of the museum – I intended to work according to what
may be called pedagogical ends. I was attracted by the idea
of definitively introducing a new aesthetic genre among us.'[6]

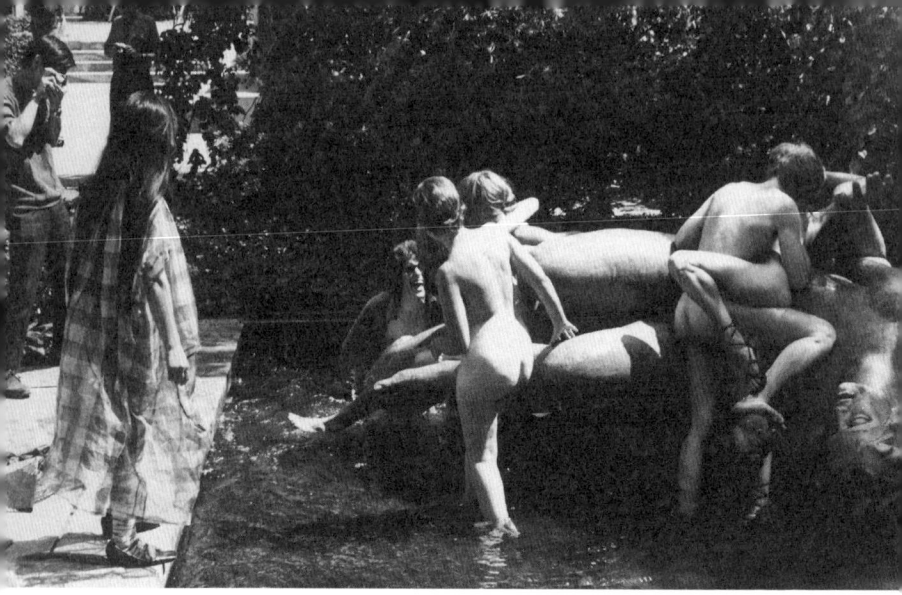

Fig.3   Yayoi Kusama, *Grand Orgy to Awaken the Dead at Moma
(Otherwise known as the Museum of Modern Art) Featuring their usual display
of nudes*, The Museum of Modern Art, New York, 24 August 1969

The presence of performance in the museum raised
the issue of its institutional validation. This question was
confronted, more or less explicitly, by artists mimicking
the conventions of sculpture, thus positioning performance
in relation to an established medium. As the human body
enjoys a three-dimensional presence in museums in stone,
bronze or marble, some artists involved in performance found
in sculpture a distant cousin through whom they could gauge
the legitimacy of their performance pieces as works of art.
This kinship was materialised with plinths, on which Pi Lind
placed actual people of various social types at the Moderna
Museet in Stockholm (*Living Sculptures*, 1967), and Oscar Bony
planted a whole family of three at the Instituto Torcuato
Di Tella (*La familia obrera* [The Working-Class Family], 1968,
fig.5). As for Gilbert and George, not only did they paint their
faces and hands to appear like bronze but they pushed further
the analogy with sculpture by standing still for a whole day
at the Stedelijk Museum in Amsterdam in 1969. A feeling

of inadequacy was perhaps conveyed by the two artists choosing to present their *Living Sculpture* in the grand stairs of the museum, that is to say in a passageway which was clearly not intended for the display of art.

The analogy of performance with sculpture was also used by Yayoi Kusama when, in 1969, she instructed eight performers to strip off and strike poses echoing sculptures on display in the garden of the Museum of Modern Art in New York for *Grand Orgy to Awaken the Dead at Moma* (fig.3). The performers flaunted their liveness under the nose of sculptures, among them Aristide Maillol's *La Rivière* (The River, 1943), a large naked female figure lying on a low pedestal in the middle of a shallow pool of water, her twisted body and raised arms offering surfaces to lean on and bumps and curves to hold on to. As for Kusama, in a nod to the museum, she read a statement titled 'Thoughts on the Mausoleum of Modern Art'. *Grand Orgy to Awaken the Dead at Moma* was unannounced and unauthorised, and the ambivalence of this forceful institutional embrace of performance would come to encapsulate its relationship with the museum.

BITING THE HAND OF THE MUSEUM

Unruly Behaviour

The institutionalisation of performance took place in the 1960s against the background of social and political dissent. Riots erupted in Paris in May 1968 and, in the same period, protests against repressive regimes intensified in Brazil, Mexico and Czechoslovakia, while in the United States the escalation of the Vietnam War prompted demonstrations and violent clashes with the police. In such context, the museum, with its administration and hierarchy, its authority to include and to exclude, and its power to orchestrate consecrations and validate new trends, had often been cast in the role of an agent of control. 'I'm put off by museums in general', claimed Allan Kaprow in 1967, 'they reek of a holy death which offends my sense of reality'.[7] Patricia

Falguières explains that with the development of Institutional Critique from the 1970s, the art institution tended to be perceived through the prism of normativity and the imposition of oppressive rules. In her analysis, 'the norm, finally localized, identified, named, was described as that limit that established itself in full force, providing bounds of prohibition and repression to objects and practices to which it remained exterior, an abusive container that entrapped art's spontaneous practices'.[8]

It was not the objective of the museum to repress live performance with institutional rules. But in the face of artists claiming their freedom and inclined to take charge of the presentation of their works, the interest of the museum in performance could be seen as an opportunity to gain exposure and recognition as much as a potential existential threat. Often loosely scripted and prone to outbursts of improvisation, performance seemed particularly unruly for the highly regulated place that is the museum. Its artistic licence and freedom to behave according to its own rules were epitomised in Jean-Jacques Lebel's aptly titled festivals of 'free expression', in which social conventions and rules of decency were commonly abused (for example, when a group of scantily clad performers engaged in sensual promiscuity in Carolee Schneemann's *Meat Joy* in 1964). The first editions took place at the American Center in Paris until the director was dismissed in 1965 because of the scandal caused by Lebel's *Déchirex*, in which nudity and sex left little room for veiled ambiguity.

The not so uncommon intervention of the authorities reinforced the thrust of performance as an unruly form of art. Both Jean-Jacques Lebel and Gustav Metzger had to report to the police because of the activities that took place at their festivals, and Nam June Paik and Charlotte Moorman the same because of *Opera Sextronique* (1967), in which the latter played the cello naked from the waist up. Günter Brus's walk performance *Wiener Spaziergang* was prematurely terminated by the police in Vienna in 1965, and three years later the artist was sentenced to a six-month prison term for public indecency in *Kunst und Revolution* (Art and Revolution), at the University

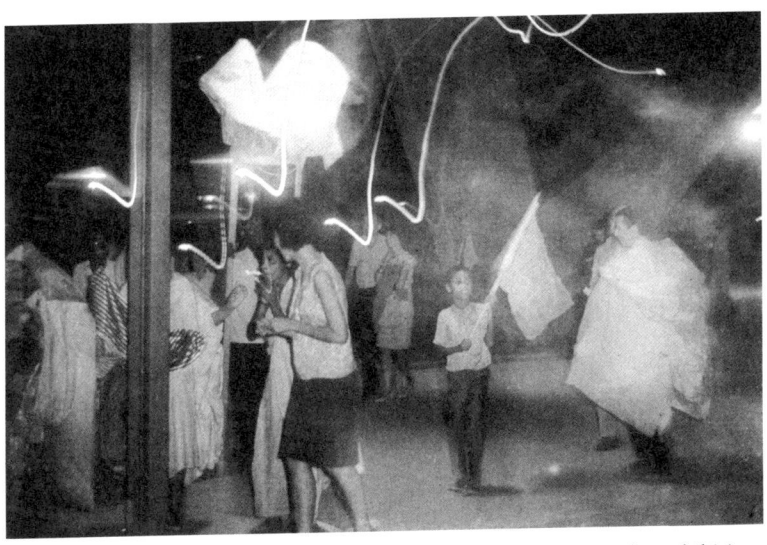

Fig.4   Hélio Oiticica, *Inauguration of Parangolé*, performance at the exhibition *Opinião '65*, Museu de Arte Moderna, Rio de Janeiro, 1965

of Vienna, in which he urinated in public and drank his urine, among other actions (Brus fled the country to avoid jail). Such episodes were striking enough to play a significant part in consolidating the distinctiveness of performance as being unfit for institutional presentation.

The institutionalisation of performance could be perceived as its compliance to the norms of museum display and its placement in a clinical institution keeping misbehaviour under control. At a time when the architectural container of art was increasingly taking the form of a pristine white cube, paving the way for what Brian O'Doherty would later describe as 'the placelessness and timelessness of the gallery's hysterical cell',[9] the ability of the museum to accommodate performance was put into question not only in the context of its role as a public institution, but also as an exhibition space. This incompatibility seemed confirmed when, in 1965, dancers wearing capes, tents and banners were recruited from the *favelas* by Hélio Oiticica to perform *Inauguration of Parangolé* at the opening of the exhibition *Opinião '65* (Opinion '65) at the Museu de Arte Moderna in Rio de Janeiro (fig.4), but were barred from the exhibition after entering the museum. Whether the exclusion was due to the possible risks posed to other exhibits by the performers, the fact that they were not on the official guest list, or the social disparity between people from the slums and the other attendees, it amounted to abrupt and unequivocal censorship.

Soon after the *Opinião '65* incident, Oiticica developed a markedly anti-institutional rhetoric which made explicit his suspicion that the museum was not able, or not willing, to adapt to unfixed and impermanent forms of art. His body of sculptures called *Parangolé* was 'an anti-art par excellence', he wrote in 1966, before claiming that he intended to make 'things which would not be transportable, but which I would invite the public to participate in. This would be a fatal blow to the concept of the museum, art gallery, etc., and to the very concept of "exhibition".'[10] Audience participation exposes the museum to the risk of losing control over people's actions, a possibility that was all the more of a threat in a military dictatorship such as that which gripped Brazil at the time. Despite his uncompromising stance, Oiticica would present works in museums with his *Penetraveis*, a series of environments that could be visited by spectators. His ambiguous relationship with the museum is perhaps best illustrated by *Apocalipopótese*, which he organised with Rogerio Duarte in 1968. Several artists, among them Lygia Pape, whose plastic sculpture *O ovo* (The Egg, 1967) was pierced by participants to simulate the act of being born, participated in this series of artistic interventions which took place in the same neighbourhood as the Museu de Arte Moderna in Rio de Janeiro, but outside, as if thumbing one's nose at the institution.

Acting Out Dissent

Acting out resistance against the museum appeared as an act of political activism. At stake were the integrity and power of the artist, formulated through a rhetoric of independence (art does not need the museum to exist) or asserted in a display of renunciation (severing the ties with the museum). At the opening of the exhibition *Experiencias '68*, curated by Patricia Rizzo at the Instituto Torcuato Di Tella in Buenos Aires in May 1968, visitors were greeted by Pablo Suárez who, in lieu of showing a work in the exhibition (whose invitation he had declined), stood at the door of the museum and distributed copies of his 'Letter of Resignation'. He noted in this message, 'is it important to do something inside the institution, even though it contributes to its destruction?'[11] A turbulent event, the opening of the exhibition ended with a number of artists taking their works out of the Di Tella after Roberto Plate's *Baño* (Bathroom), an installation which visitors could enter and whose walls were gradually covered with graffiti, part of it against the regime, was sealed by the police. Oscar Bony, who participated in the show with the display of a working-class family (fig.5), later declared, 'At the time we believed in a utopia that finally proved to be impossible: the possibility of obviating galleries and museums'.[12] In 1971 he would decline an invitation to participate in an exhibition at the Camden Art Centre in London, instead inserting a statement in the catalogue that read, 'I am in favour of non-participation as being true avant-garde'.[13]

Declining an invitation to participate in an exhibition, or withdrawing one's work, and making this public, was performing an act of refusal to comply with an institution suspected of authoritarianism or artistic conservatism. Such gestures also signalled that the reciprocal relation of interest between the artist and the museum was broken. Contesting against the museum gained credence as a prominent statement of artistic and political probity, and this stance could apply to artists working in any medium. In 1969 Takis removed one of his works on display in the exhibition *The Machine as Seen at the End of the Mechanical Age* at the Museum of Modern Art in New York because he disapproved of the choice of that particular work for the show (even if the museum, as the owner of the piece, was not required to consult him). Accompanied by friends and fellow artists, Takis took his work to the museum garden and staged a sit-in.

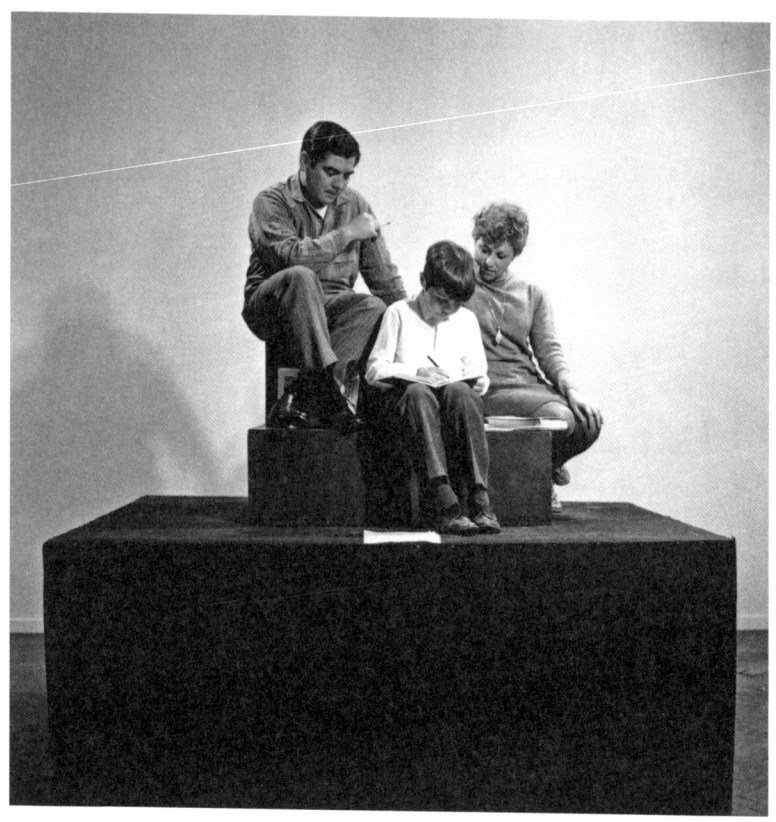

Fig.5 Oscar Bony, *La familia obrera* (The Working-Class Family), 1968, performance at the exhibition *Experiencias '68*, Instituto Torcuato Di Tella, Buenos Aires, May 1968

Another act of dissent happened at the Museum of Modern Art in New York when in 1970 the newly founded Art Workers' Coalition asked to remove Pablo Picasso's *Guernica* (1937) from view as a gesture of opposition to the Vietnam War. Following the museum's decision not to comply, a protest was organised in the museum, in front of the painting. With flowers laid at the feet of the work, posters showing Vietnamese victims, texts read aloud and opinions voiced through a megaphone, the action stood halfway between political protest and performance. Such interventions were an echo chamber of the global political turmoil, and they made the disruptive potential of performance very clear. As writer and curator Lucy R. Lippard has noted, 'almost universally, artists pin their hopes on institutional support as a passport to the future',[14] although, she adds, the museum is 'both the hand that feeds and the citadel to be stormed'.[15]

As a medium of short existence, performance proved particularly sensitive to the evolution of its relationship with the art institution. A gulf appeared between artists welcoming the invitation of the museum and those, concerned about potential pitfalls and manipulation, to whom such embrace was anathema. The first time a live performance was presented at the then Tate Gallery, in London, highlighted a polarisation of stances. The sculptor César was having considerable success by making sculptures with liquid polyurethane (a synthetic resin which hardens quickly) before an audience, when he was invited by the museum to present a live session of *Expansions* in 1968. Although in France he cultivated the persona of a working-class and non-intellectual artist, in the eyes of Stuart Brisley, who was himself involved in performance and César's junior of twelve years, he was the embodiment of the institution-sanctioned artist. As the French sculptor cut solidified resin into pieces in a vast gallery, signed them and gave them away to spectators, Brisley, who attended the event along with fellow artist Peter Sedgley, took chunks of the sculpture to the museum yard, stuck them on the railings and set them on fire. The arson, billed as a performance in its own right (it was proudly listed as an 'Unofficial action' in the catalogue of Brisley's solo exhibition in 1981[16]), allowed him to assert his own transgressive persona, in opposition to the 'official' culture symbolised by the celebrated artist, the museum and its clique.

Brisley crashing the official party, not quite smuggling his own work into the museum but staging it just outside, is symptomatic of another direction taken by artists in resistance to the institution. Rather than shunning the museum altogether, some artists developed dynamic strategies of opposition from within, pressing their own agenda and imposing their own terms for the presentation of live works. Exhibition openings proved a formidable stage for unannounced works, as turning oneself into art is a privilege specific to performance. Gilbert and George, who were unhappy not to have been selected for the London instalment of the exhibition *Live in Your Head: When Attitudes Become Form (Works – Concepts – Processes – Situations – Information)* in 1969, presented themselves as 'living sculptures' at the opening at the Institute of Contemporary Arts. Echoing this episode, Antonio Manuel attended the opening of the exhibition *XIX National Salon of Modern Art* at the Museu de Arte Moderna in Rio de Janeiro in 1970 and suddenly stripped naked, climbed the stairs and stood on a parapet holding on to a pole. This action, entitled *O corpo é a obra* (The Body Is a Work of Art), was made in response to the rejection by the jury of his original proposal for the show, consisting in his body as a work of art. *O corpo é a obra* was performed in a country under dictatorship, where there was 'a climate of fear, and even when artists were not directly persecuted they suffered under self-imposed censorship'.[17] Exempt from the limitations of official consent, this unauthorised performance flaunted its utter freedom in a siege of power.

THE EXHIBITION

A Slot for Live Works

The inclusion of live works in museum exhibitions also met with practical obstacles. Live action tends to need space, not only to accommodate performers but also an audience and, in the context of an exhibition, this can easily pose a risk to other works placed nearby. In addition, a performance occurs at a particular time, requiring specific administration of the venue and of visitors that is foreign to the display of objects. And the duration of exhibitions over several months is much less suited to performance than festivals are. The curatorial idiosyncrasy of live artworks tests both the flexibility of performance to adapt to the constraints of the exhibition format, and the capacity of the exhibition to accommodate performance within its spatial and temporal configuration.

The period in between exhibitions was often the interstice through which live performance made its way to the museum, emptied galleries and special opening times facilitating the process. In 1969 Meredith Monk was given the whole atrium of the Solomon R. Guggenheim Museum in New York for one day to show *Juice: A Theatre Cantata in Three Installments*, the first live work to be presented in the institution. *Juice* was conceived specifically for this museum, and on the ramp of the atrium a cast of no fewer than 75 performers was visible to the audience gathered at the bottom. Most of them were dressed in white with red boots (just four were dressed in red). They dispersed into small groups, prompting the audience to move throughout the space. In the same period, the Whitney Museum of American Art in New York also used its space for live events between shows, as curator Jay Sanders has explained: 'Curators Marcia Tucker and James Monte were aware of what was happening in alternative spaces and lofts in the late 1960s and early 1970s, and realized that they could offer comparable conditions for performance by clearing the museum's galleries of their objects and walls.'[18]

The inauguration of an exhibition has probably been the solution the museum has the most frequently opted for to display live works. While it has offered an opportunity to include and frame a live event as a component of a show, it has also restricted it to a specific moment. At the opening of *Experiencias '68* in Buenos Aires, Juan Stoppani's *Todo lo que Juan Stoppani no se pudo poner* (Everything that Juan Stoppani Could not Wear, 1968) was performed by a woman wearing a dress and a very long blue satin turban running along the floor through the space, who invited the spectators to eat green apples spread around her. If it was uncommon for performance to be accommodated within the duration of an exhibition, as a unique event it took advantage of the crowd at the exhibition opening, as well as the museum's extended hours and the presence of additional staff. Repeating the performance hit obvious logistical problems, and it was all the more remarkable that Bony's *La familia obrera* (fig.5) was shown throughout *Experiencias '68*, the live display of the woman, man and child who constituted the work being maintained for the ten days of the exhibition.

Displaying Objects or Live Works

Among the problems posed by exhibitions on performance, the question of the presentation of past works is particularly thorny. While Allan Kaprow reflected in 1966 that his book *Assemblage, Environments & Happenings* was written 'in the midst of a young activity',[19] he was also aware that performance was starting to have a history, however brief. The need to keep a record of past events was tackled early on by the very protagonists of this history. Wolf Vostell wrote *Happenings, Fluxus, Pop Art, Nouveau Réalisme: Eine Dokumentation* with Jürgen Becker in 1965 and Claes Oldenburg collaborated with Emmet Williams on *Store Days: Documents from The Store (1961) and Ray Gun Theater (1962)* in 1967;[20] both publications give prime importance to documents. Kaprow's 1966 book itself contains a good number of photographs, highlighting the particular significance of documentation in making the history of performance. This approach reflects that of the museum when its first task in the preparation of an exhibition is to fish for ephemera and documents. Posters, props, notes, photographs and videos are not just useful for research, they are also potential display material.

In exhibitions, a way of broadening the range of items addressing the history of performance and not being confined to the display of archives is to evoke performance as a central player in a broader alternative scene that also includes, for example, ephemeral works or works involving audience participation or motion. This method guided the conception of *Eleven from the Reuben Gallery*, an exhibition mounted in 1965 at the Guggenheim Museum in New York in honour of the then defunct gallery, which had been central to the emergence of performance, as well as installations, in New York in the early 1960s. In this show devoted to a short-lived gallery that partly made its name through ephemeral artworks, focus was placed on permanent works such as sculptures (by Claes Oldenburg, George Segal and Robert Whitman), objects susceptible to being used, including a case of objects by George Brecht (*The Case*, 1959), and a series of instructions for a happening by Kaprow inscribed on a piece of cardboard (*Raining*, 1965).

From the late 1960s, important exhibitions tackling performance indicated various possible strategies for such an exercise. When in 1967 the Museum of Contemporary Art in Chicago conceived its inaugural exhibition, *Pictures to be Read / Poetry to be Seen*, around performance, it sent a strong message about its ambition to confront the experimental edge of contemporary art and also the curatorial challenges posed by it (the museum would soon reaffirm this aspiration by hosting the premiere of Carolee Schneemann's group performance *Illinois Central* in January 1968). *Pictures to be Read / Poetry to be Seen* included a number of works by artists associated with performance and Fluxus (among them George Brecht, Öyvind Fahlström, Ray Johnson, Alison Knowles and Wolf Vostell) around the theme of the intersection between language and images. On display were a few scripts of performances, while a variety of objects evoked the broader landscape of works based on process and participation, for example Kaprow's *Words* (1962), an installation requiring the manipulation of the audience.

Symptomatic of the curatorial conundrum posed by performance was the fact that live performance was presented in a separate exhibition, which was organised in conjunction with *Pictures to be Read / Poetry to be Seen* and opened a month later in the same museum. Called *Two Happening Concepts: Allan Kaprow and Wolf Vostell* and concentrating on two key figures, one from the United States and the other from Europe, the show was itself divided into two distinct parts proposing contrasting formats for exhibitions on performance. The section on Vostell adopted an archive-oriented approach by focusing on documents such as photographs, preparatory drawings and scripts. Vostell's experience of gathering documentation, as he did for his book, facilitated such an approach (which was also that taken in his first solo exhibition, *Wolf Vostell: Bilder Verwischungen Happening-Notationen 1961–1966* [Images Blur Happening-Notations] at Kölnischer Kunstverein in Cologne in 1966). By contrast, the section devoted to Kaprow consisted exclusively of one live work. *Moving* (1967) was a new piece that took place over four days, not inside the museum but in different parts of Chicago. The performance, in which old furniture was pushed through the streets, was dedicated to Milan Knížák. It echoed performances presented by the Czech artist in the streets of Prague during the Communist period, when works executed in the outdoor space were hard to track down and thereby mitigated against government control. Ostensibly, *Moving* spoke of Kaprow's suspicion of institutional constraints and his reluctance to confine live performance to the museum.

Kaprow's notoriety as a pioneer of performance led him to be courted by museums to an extent that is probably unequal to any other protagonists of historic performance. As he gained extensive exposure, he seemed to set himself a code of conduct intended to safeguard live works by keeping them at a distance from the museum. This is not to say that he shunned the museum altogether. In his first major solo exhibition, at Pasadena Art Museum in 1967, his material production was given ample room within the museum with collages, assemblages and environments, while a new happening, *Fluids*, was presented in the open air, in different locations around Pasadena and Los Angeles. *Fluids* required participants to make rectangular structures with ice bricks and ice, a work that contradicted the museum imperatives of permanence and of a contained form. As analysed by curator Eva Meyer-Hermann, 'This endeavour to construct transient forms in the warm California sun can be read as an attempt to symbolically deconstruct the museum. The edifices literally melted away.'[21]

When Harald Szeemann decided to dedicate an exhibition
to *Happening & Fluxus* in Cologne in 1970, he made a point
of concentrating as closely as possible on performance. In the
curator's view, 'happenings' represented not only the New York
scene revolving around Allan Kaprow but, more generally,
visual artists engaged in performance (a term which would
only become widely used from the early 1970s). As for Fluxus,
it indicated a loose network of artists yet a clearly identifiable
movement. Before *Happening & Fluxus* there had been no real
precedent of exhibitions charting the history of performance
with such focus. Szeemann handled this project while being
very mindful of the role of the museum, and the relationship
it established with artists. In preparing his landmark exhibition
When Attitudes Become Form at the Kunsthalle Bern the
previous year, he had noted, 'The exhibition really shouldn't
simply reinforce the idea of the museum as a temple, but rather
bear witness to the fact that, done in the same spirit, different
things can develop'.[22] In Bern, the critique of the museum that
pervaded contemporary art practices was evident, for example
when Jan Dibbets dug trenches around the Kunsthalle building
in order to expose its foundations (*Museum Plinth with Four
Corners at an Angle of 90°*, 1969).

Committed to a conception of the museum as a place that
should be sympathetic to art based on process, Szeemann's
curatorial approach consisted in inviting artists rather than
selecting existing works. This has been described by Jean-Marc
Poinsot as a 'strategy of non-involvement towards an artist's
action [which] became a model for collective events' around
that time.[23] The Bern exhibition had not featured any live
works within the museum, but it prompted Szeemann to start
working on his new show focusing on performance. In doing
so, he was aware he was taking a pretty unexplored path.
He wrote to George Brecht in January 1970, 'The good thing
with [the Bern exhibition] ... was: it gave me courage to suggest
the more difficult task to make an exhibition on Happenings

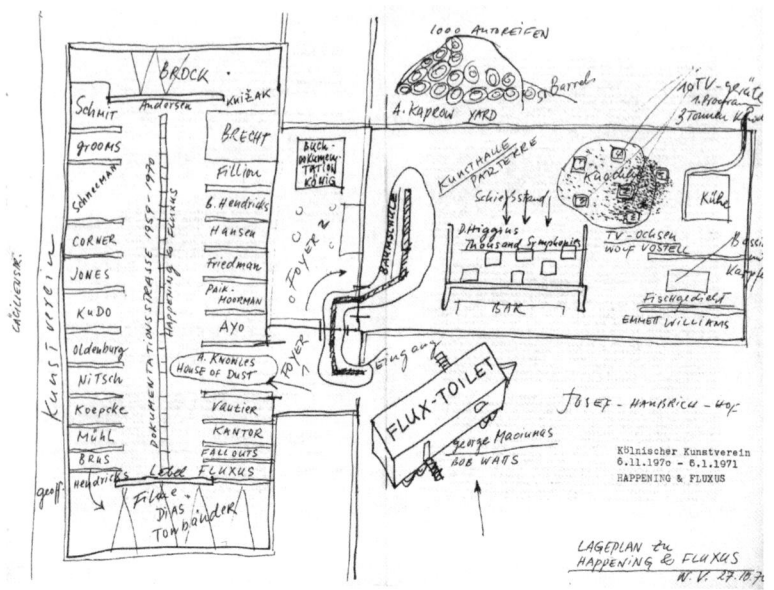

Fig.6   Wolf Vostell, floor plan of the exhibition *Happening & Fluxus*, 1970, reproduced in *Dokumentationstrasse Checklist and 'Happening & Fluxus' Brochure with drawing by Wolf Vostell*, 1971, bound volume, 22.2 × 14.16 × 0.5 cm (8 ¾ × 5 ¾ × ³⁄₁₆ in.)

and Fluxus which I discovered through [the artists in *When Attitudes Become Form*]'.[24]

As the exhibition promised to be a 'difficult task', Szeemann requested the help of Vostell, whom he saw as a 'happening veteran'.[25] *Happening & Fluxus* opened at the Kölnischer Kunstverein in Cologne in 1970, and it was unique in its ambition to combine and interweave different curatorial approaches (fig.6). A large number of documents from 1959 to 1970 gathered by Hanns Sohm, a collector of Fluxus memorabilia, were displayed in a vitrine and on panels called the 'Documentation Path'. In addition, each artist was assigned an individual section which could be used either to show documentation of past works, as for Claes Oldenburg, or to display new ones made for the exhibition. Some artists used their individual space to create installations, which resulted, in a few cases, in works falling neither into the 'happening'

PERFORMANCE IN THE MUSEUM

nor into the 'Fluxus' categories, performance ending up being represented through its protagonists rather than as the medium itself. For example, Carolee Schneemann filled her section with mirrors, slide projections and television broadcasts, with sheets of paper hanging from the walls and detergent having been spread on the floor (*Meat System 1: Electronic Activation Room*, 1970).

Happening & Fluxus included a programme of live performances, and Szeemann was keen to work on it until the last moment. He explained later that the list of works was deliberately not included in the catalogue so he would be 'more free'.[26] While Ben Vautier and Charlotte Moorman performed live pieces in the main section of the exhibition, Allan Kaprow insisted on his performance *Sawdust* being presented in the non-artistic setting of a local carpentry shop. As for Vostell, he delegated the execution of his performance to a pregnant cow that was expected to give birth during the run of the exhibition (*Kuh* [Cow], 1970), something which had not been authorised by the authorities. In addition, a number of live works took place in an adjacent space during a three-day event kicking off at the exhibition opening. The live programme was somewhat dominated by the Viennese Actionists, not only with Hermann Nitsch's *O.M. Theater* (1970) but also Otto Muehl's *Manopsychotic Ballet* (1970), the naked performers in the latter immediately sparking controversy.

Happening & Fluxus was marred with difficulties, among them Vostell threatening to boycott the exhibition when authorisation of the display of the cow was declined. Szeemann wrote to the art dealer John Gibson, 'This exhibition, I'm afraid to tell, will be the last one where I give artists the opportunity to do what they like. All these museums and so on are not built for the kind of exhibitions I like and artists – there are always exceptions – don't understand it, what I understand, too.'[27] Szeemann, however, persevered in his attempt to curate performance on the occasion of his appointment as curator of *Documenta V*, in Kassel in 1972, where a whole section named 'Individual Mythologies' gave ample room to bodyworks such as photographs by Rudolf Schwarzkogler, and to live works by Joseph Beuys (*Office for Direct Democracy through Referendum*, 1972), Rebecca Horn (*Head Extension*, 1972), Gustav Metzger (*Karba*, 1970–2), Klaus Rinke (*Primary Demonstration*, 1972) and several performances by James Lee Byars, among other artists.

Vito Acconci, Institutional Irritant

From the late 1960s, performance was an essential cog of the conceptual turn taken by art practices based on concepts, principles and procedures. The contemporary art scene became dominated by works, as Lucy Lippard has written, 'in which the idea is paramount and the material form is secondary, lightweight, ephemeral, cheap, unpretentious, and / or "dematerialized"'.[28] Such an evolution in art-making had repercussions for the very nature of artworks and their presentation in exhibitions. For example, Richard Long's contribution to *When Attitudes Become Form* was a walk he did in the mountains, which was notified by a poster displayed in the Kunsthalle Bern (*A Walking Tour in the Berner Oberland*, 1969), with both material and immaterial components comprising the work. Most importantly, with the advent of Conceptual Art came a critique of the institution as art practice. By contrast with artists storming out of the museum to make their insubordination clear and visible, performance adopting the posture of Institutional Critique operated within the museum.

Conceptual Art was surveyed in the large exhibition *Information*, curated by Kynaston McShine at the Museum of Modern Art in New York in 1970. Invited to contribute to the show, Vito Acconci, who had only recently oriented his practice from poetry towards the visual arts, chose to present a live performance. For his first engagement with a museum exhibition, he had his mail forwarded by post to the Museum of Modern Art and left on a table placed among other exhibits, along with a statement describing the principle of the piece (*Service Area*, 1970). He appeared at the exhibition just to pick up the mail and leave the table empty, or alternatively chose not to turn up and leave the mail piling up. Daily routine was not foreign to his practice as he engaged with regular repetition in *Following Piece* (1969), among other works. However, *Service Area* was extremely mundane and offered none of the psychological tension or the physical endurance which often characterised his art at the time. Instead, strain was put on the museum, which was reduced to being a mere service provider.

The design of the *Information* exhibition was notable for ample empty space, as documents and images were present in much greater numbers than three-dimensional works – a presentation that reflected art privileging concept over materiality. Acconci may have had this spaciousness in mind when he conceived *Proximity Piece* (1970) two months later for *Software – Information Technology: Its New Meaning for Art* (Jewish Museum, New York, 1970), another exhibition on Conceptual Art. Playing against roomy exhibition space, he chose to 'crowd people' and quietly stand close enough to them to disturb their contemplation, induce a sense of awkwardness and, in all probability, prompt them to move away. This disruption of the free circulation of the visitors was repeated eight hours a day during the 52 days the exhibition was open. Through uneasy personal interactions, the artist cast himself, in his own words, in the role of the 'performer [who] can become the parasite on the party',[29] a strategy of individual agency within the public domain which was shared by other artists at the time, including Adrian Piper with her series *Catalysis* (1970–3).

Acconci's contributions to *Information* and *Software* were remarkable in their use of the temporal and spatial structure of the exhibition. On one hand, the artist demonstrated a striking compliance to this structure by enabling his performances to fill the entire duration of the exhibitions and by occupying the same space as material works. On the other hand, he assumed the role of institutional irritant, as *Service Area* was governed by its own unpredictable and whimsical timing and *Proximity*

Piece thwarted the circulation of visitors in the galleries. Time and space were compelling coordinates to engage with the structural limitations of the exhibition and expose it as a highly regulated apparatus. Both works highlighted the rules, regulations and control inherent in the institution, something that is addressed with particular prescience in *Service Area* as the museum was assigned the task of policing the mail. 'Because', Acconci wrote, 'the mail is at the museum, on exhibit, the museum guard's normal services are used to guard against a "federal offence": his function shifts to that of a mail guard.'[30]

The dual axis of space and time was central to Michel Foucault's definition of discipline as a modern way of controlling the body in institutions such as prisons, hospitals and factories. Among the characteristics of 'disciplinary institutions' enclosed upon themselves, as analysed by the philosopher in 1975, are the distribution of bodies in assigned spaces and an exhaustion of the use of time as a 'principle of non-idleness'.[31] The adaptation of performance to the spatial and temporal constraints of the exhibition was played out by Acconci only to be simultaneously contradicted. In *Information* he committed to appear in the museum to collect his mail, yet he might equally have a break. In *Software* he ensured his presence throughout the whole exhibition and yet he forced a circulation within the galleries which was determined by emotional disruption rather than practical navigation. Space and time were used to act out the indocile institutionalisation of performance and flaunt its capacity to disturb the order of the museum. These parameters were used to the same effect when Mierle Laderman Ukeles locked doors between galleries of The Wadsworth Atheneum in Hartford, Connecticut, trapping visitors in portions of the building (*The Keeping of the Keys: Maintenance as Security*, 1973), and when Chris Burden lay still, behind a large sheet of glass, on the floor of the Museum of Contemporary Art in Chicago, leaving the staff in the dark about his plan, prompting them to open late in order not to interrupt the work, and only ending the performance after 45 hours (*Doomed*, 1975).

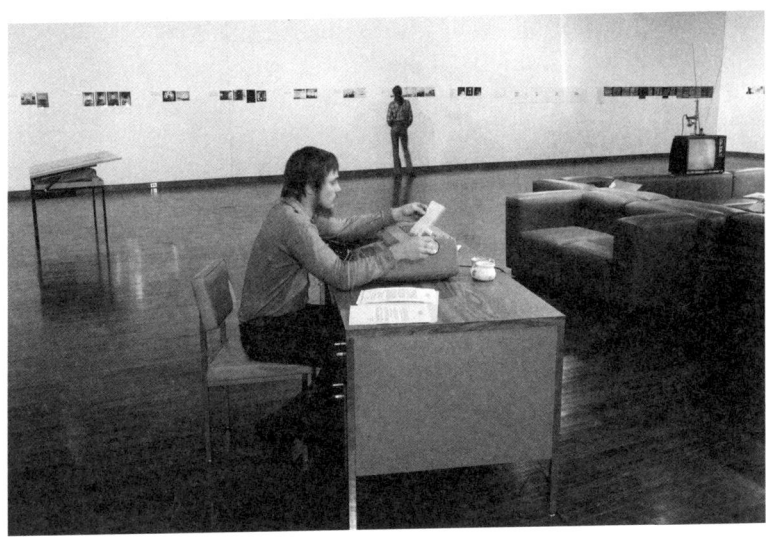

Fig.7   Chris Burden, *Working Artist*, 1975,
University of Maryland Gallery, Baltimore

THE PERFORMANCE ARTIST AT WORK

The situation of 'Performance and the Arts' was discussed
in 1975 in a panel organised by the College Art Association
in Washington D.C. and coordinated by Allan Kaprow.
Reporting on this event, and more specifically on the role
played by performance and the Judson Dance Theater in the
1960s, Andrée Hayum wrote: 'those performances left a wake
of viewers struggling for comprehension ... At the same time
a small but staunch group of supporters did develop which
was encouraging for all concerned. But characteristic of
an audience of the faithful is that it becomes all-accepting,
that it learns what to expect. This is one of the predicaments
these artists face in 1975.'[32]

That year, Chris Burden reflected on his career, still short
but already notorious for unsettling performances involving
physical and psychological strain, in the solo show *Working
Artist* held at the University of Maryland Gallery in Baltimore
(fig.7). Photographs of past performances accompanied by texts

were displayed on the walls of the spacious gallery. The photographs were fixed on the wall with pins of a type one would expect to find in offices, juxtaposed with minimum space between them. They were all printed at the same size and aligned along their top edge, whether horizontally or vertically oriented. Some adjoining photographs differed only slightly, either in their framing or in their printing in black and white or in colour. The systematic selection of documents and their matter-of-fact display seemed to dismiss the deployment of any curatorial skill or imagination, evoking a catalogue rather than an art exhibition.

Working Artist was also a performance, involving the artist *at work*, which took place over three days in the same exhibition space. A desk, a telephone, a typewriter, a television and a drafting table accompanied sofas in the centre of the gallery so Burden could live in this domestic setting during the opening hours, napping on a couch, watching television, conducting his daily affairs, greeting visitors and chatting with them as if they were his guests. So ordinary were these daily routine actions that the performance was barely discernible as such. In fact, the nondescriptness of the action stood in sharp contrast with the actions captured in the surrounding photographs, for example one showing the artist, only a few years younger, standing dazed and deathly pale after he was shot in the forearm (*Shoot*, 1971). To the image of the radical and uncompromising artist conveyed in his performances was now opposed the iconography of a 'working artist' performing routine administrative tasks and managing his career between naps and television breaks in the homely environment of the museum.

Chapter 2

Conservation: Reviving Past Performance Works, 1980s–2000s

In 1980 Chris Burden referred to his own history in one of his last performances, *Show the Hole*. To members of the audience individually invited to join him in a booth, the artist talked about his piece *Shoot* (1971). He reminisced about the event that resulted in a bullet being lodged in his arm (instead of grazing it as planned) and showed the scar left as a result. Playing with his mythology as a radical artist (and alluding to the incredulity of the Apostle Thomas), Burden made the posterity of the piece the very subject of a new work. Putting himself in charge of caring for the memory of *Shoot*, he carried out the job in the mode of a personal and intimate one-to-one encounter that no documentation could match.

By the time Burden revisited this seminal work, the vast majority of artists of his generation who were involved in performance had given up doing live works. As these pioneers got older and tended to move away from performance, a sense took hold that the 'Golden Years' of performance, as RoseLee Goldberg dubbed them in 1984,[1] had passed. With the early history of performance receding into the distance, the question arose of how to display previous performance works in exhibitions. It was during this period, in the 1980s, that the idea of the somewhat implausible business that is the conservation of performance started to emerge.

The terms of the conservation of performance were at first largely articulated in the context of exhibitions. Rather than a matter arising from the care of museum collections, this kind of conservation grew out of curatorial propositions. From the 1980s, a prevalent pattern of behaviour in museums was the reconstruction of objects pertaining to performance, revolving around elastic ideas of replication. In parallel and sometimes as a reaction against object reconstructions, live actions started to be repeated and re-enacted. Concluding this period of reflection on the regeneration of performance, special emphasis was placed, after 2000, on the role of documentation. This array of practices was initiated or encouraged by the museum, which provided material, logistical, financial and documentary assistance. Often pragmatically driven and sometimes theoretically perilous, these practices started to shape the parameters of the conservation of performance.

RECONSTRUCTIONS

A Centrifugal Curatorial Approach

Jean-Marc Poinsot has noted that from around 1980, 'certain museums and exhibition organizers demonstrated the need to advance the writing of history, proposing appraisals which could redistribute works and events' in the form of 'huge sweeping exhibition[s]' and other 'monumental compilations'.[2] At first, performance featured parsimoniously in these surveys, until in the 1990s large museum exhibitions set themselves the task of mapping out its history. The size, encyclopaedic ambition, and broad geographical and chronological scopes of these shows speak to the drive for comprehensive curatorial approaches to the history of performance. As an institution whose primary reason for being is the collection and display of tangible artefacts, the museum's response to historical performance was at first articulated through the prism of the object.

Hors limites: L'art et la vie, 1952–1994 (Off Limits: Art and Life, 1952–1994), held at the Centre Pompidou in Paris in 1994–5, was an ambitious and sweeping survey, one of the first of its kind. A mammoth exhibition curated by Jean de Loisy, it spread over two galleries on both sides of the central atrium while a new sculpture by Jean-Jacques Lebel was commissioned for the atrium. The history of performance was charted over four decades with a wealth of photographs, videos, sculptures and various works by artists such as VALIE EXPORT, Gilbert and George, Allan Kaprow, Urs Lüthi, Orlan and Carolee Schneemann. These artists had in common, François Barré wrote in the exhibition catalogue, the desire to overcome 'the contemplation of the masterpiece or the object' in favour of 'actions' and works which could be ephemeral.[3]

In an approach which originated in the 1960s and gained considerable credence at the time of *Hors limites*, the history of performance was intertwined with that of ephemeral installations and forms of art toying with movement or immateriality. This centrifugal approach to performance, revolving around it without sticking exclusively to it, allowed not only documents but sculptures, paintings and other material works to be displayed. Conceived in this vein, *Out of Actions: Between Performance and the Object, 1949–1979* (The Geffen Contemporary at the Museum of Contemporary Art, Los Angeles, 1998) featured, amongst a variety of works, photographs of performances by Laurie Anderson, Ion Grigorescu and Tetsumi Kudo, a notebook of newspaper clippings and photographs documenting Leslie Labowitz and Suzanne Lacy's *In Mourning and in Rage* (1977), sculptures by Lygia Clark and Rebecca Horn, relics of performances by Chris Burden, and Allan Kaprow's *Yard* (1961), a large installation which visitors were invited to enter.

Rather disconcertingly, the curator of *Out of Actions*, Paul Schimmel, insisted that 'it really is not a performance show – that's one thing I was completely clear on'.[4] Such a disclaimer should be understood as an acknowledgement of the absence of live works. Schimmel's statement encapsulated the conundrum faced by exhibitions where performance was central yet live performance conspicuous, if not by its absence, then by its scarcity. This situation was less the product of curatorial philosophies than the result of material constraints and logistical difficulties. At *Hors limites* artists such as Franz West were invited to perform live before the project fell through because of budget restrictions.

In Los Angeles, Kaprow imposed such conditions on the presentation of *18 Happenings in 6 Parts*, including that the work should not be presented inside the museum and that 'The new version would be markedly different from its earliest form, but would emerge from at least 3 previous versions',[5] that the idea to include it in *Out of Actions* was abandoned. Instead, *18 Happenings in 6 Parts* was represented in the exhibition through two black-and-white photographs. As Milena Tomic has noted, 'In a 1999 letter to Schimmel, Kaprow remarked on the "humour lurking" in the title "Out of Actions", which could be read literally as "no more actions", as a gas station sign might say "out of gas"'.[6] Perhaps Michael Rush summarises best the general feeling when he asks, 'how does [an] institution, through its curatorial voice, address the significance of an ephemeral art without reducing the art to its artifacts: props, photographs, videos, sets, costumes?'[7] Frazer Ward offers a blunt answer when he asserts that 'the only definition of performance that you might derive from the exhibition [*Out of Actions*] would be that it is an attitude which seeks to equate acts of making with objects made'.[8]

Live performance which did feature in exhibitions was typically presented at openings. Eric Madeleine (then working under the name Made in Eric) lay down on the floor of *Hors limites* as an object to be stepped on, and Alexander Brener, Nenad Dančuo, Tomislav Gotovac and Jusuf Hadžifejzović all performed live works at the opening of *Body and the East: From the 1960s to the Present*, an exhibition focusing on Eastern European art which was curated by Zdenka Badovinac at Moderna galerija (Museum of Modern Art) in Ljubljana in 1998. While performances were presented at exhibition openings as a special event, remnants of these works were often shown alongside other exhibits for the rest of the show. The debris of a piano smashed by Raphael Montañez Ortiz, for example, remained on display at *Outside the Frame / Performance and the Object: A Survey of Performance in the USA since 1950* (Cleveland Center for Contemporary Art, 1994), and then again at *Out of Actions* a few years later.

The sheer number of objects produced under the auspices of Fluxus, amongst them cards, posters and publications, had long made the group a central focus of shows looking at performance.[9] This phenomenon culminated in 1993 with *In the Spirit of Fluxus*, held at the Walker Art Center in Minneapolis, which originated in a substantial acquisition by the museum of more than five hundred Fluxus items. A blessing for curators, the propensity of the movement to produce objects has also had a downside, Kristine Stiles noted in the exhibition catalogue. She wrote, 'Increasing attention by the art market and the institutions of art history to the objects, publications, and material ephemera of Fluxus threatens to erode its performative legacy'.[10] This risk is not unique to Fluxus. Generally speaking, the curatorial approach to historical performance has been largely defined by its material components. The fact that both *Out of Actions* and *Outside the Frame* included 'performance and the object' in their full titles speaks to the explicitly partisan position taken by the museum in favour of material things.

The Possibilities of Remaking

Most performances leave a trail of documents behind, and privileging this prism can appear as an obvious solution to curators. Relying primarily on documentation, however, can turn into a curatorial trap. As a reviewer of *Vito Acconci: A Retrospective 1969–1980*, held at the Museum of Contemporary Art in Chicago in 1980, has pointed out, the artist's 'conceptual / theatrical work doesn't make for a visually arresting presentation',[11] warning of the risk of visual monotony that could arise from the lining up of documents. Objects such as props and sets proved to be a salutary lifeline for curators by significantly opening up the array of exhibits stemming from performance. They could offer an engagement with past works that seemed less mediated, and an experience that felt less alienating. Orlan's solo exhibition at the Internationaal Cultureel Centrum in Antwerp in 1980, for example, included not only photographs and videos but a garment used during performances as well as life-size cut-outs of herself, standing in the gallery like perfectly still sentinels.

Far from failing to arrest attention, the Acconci retrospective in Chicago was full of meaty bits in the form of installations imitating performance sets, or fragments of them. Fabricated specially for the show, these constructions incorporated large photographs of the artist using the original sets. A photograph of him lying naked on a bed in *Reception Room* (1973) was mounted horizontally on a tabletop around which stools were placed in imitation of the material arrangement of the performance (fig.8). The combination of actual objects with images enlarged to life-size effect seemed to extend the remaking to the performer himself, albeit in two-dimensional, black-and-white form, and frozen in the position of the photograph. The overwhelming impression was that of bold curatorial imagination and an active intervention of the museum. As Acconci conceded with pragmatism, 'it's easier to do a show in a bigger place because there is more of a budget'.[12]

The possibility of retrospectively making objects pertaining to performance is also a way to ensure that the impermanence of performance is not an obstacle to its inclusion in exhibitions. For example, in 1976, sets of performances by Robert Whitman were reconstructed for *Robert Whitman: Theater Works 1960–1976* at Dia Art Foundation in New York. When Barbara Haskell was confronted by the lack of traces of ephemeral works as she curated *Blam!: The Explosion of Pop, Minimalism, and Performance 1958–1964* at the Whitney Museum in New York in 1984, she was grateful that the artists 'agreed to re-create earlier Happenings sets and environments', as she wrote, 'thereby enabling the public to experience again these transient artworks'.[13]

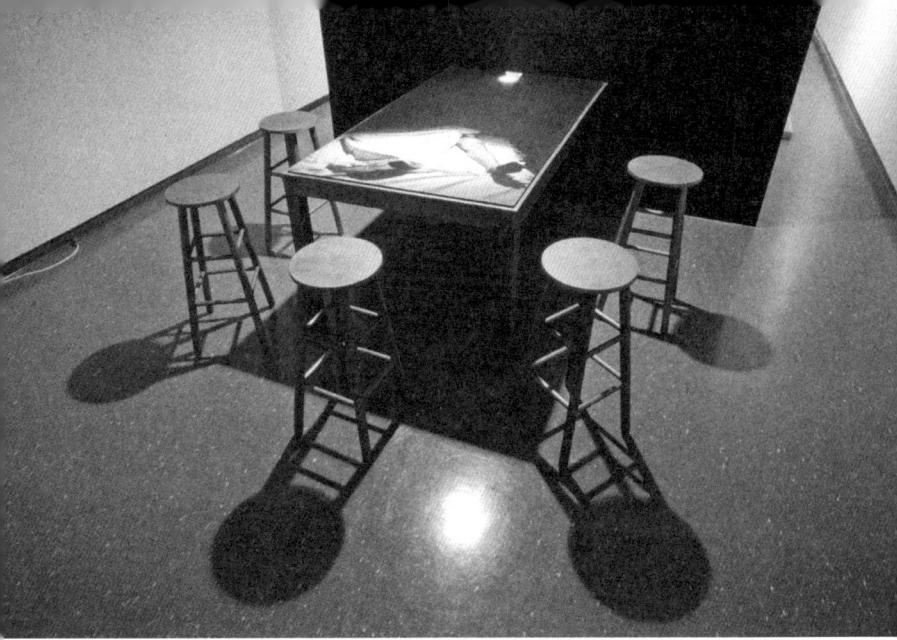

Fig.8 *Vito Acconci: A Retrospective 1969–1980*, installation view, Museum of Contemporary Art Chicago, 21 March–18 May 1980

In the section of *Blam!* devoted to performance, a huge mouth was remade with painted cloth to evoke the original set of Robert Whitman's *Mouth* (1961), a large building on fire was repainted as the set of Red Grooms's *The Burning Building* (1959) and installations by George Brecht were remade. *Blam!* was a milestone in the use of reconstructions as it used them on an unprecedented scale; it also included replicas of lost or destroyed sculptures by Robert Morris and Walter de Maria. The enthusiasm for the multifarious opportunities presented by remaking was spelt out in 1988 in the title of the exhibition *Theater of the Object: Reconstructions, Re-creations, Reconsiderations 1958–1972* at the artists-run Alternative Museum in New York, which included works by Nam June Paik, Benjamin Patterson and Carolee Schneemann recreated for the occasion.

With the refabrication of objects which did not survive live presentations, the museum found a way to flex its curatorial muscles. This exercise also applied to a significant extent to ephemeral installations. *Flux-Labyrinth*, a long installation first built at the Akademie der Künste in Berlin in 1976, which spectators were invited to enter and then walk around all sorts of obstacles, was reconstructed at *In the Spirit of Fluxus* in 1993. Similarly, installations by Hélio Oiticica were remade at his solo show at what was then the Witte de With Center for Contemporary Art in Rotterdam in 1992. Arthur Danto, however, was not impressed by the feats of reconstruction, and remarked in his review of *Blam!* that Allan Kaprow's early installations and performances were exciting partly because 'one entered them with a sense of danger', describing reconstructions as 'distancing quotations of original environments which the visitor now enters as a tourist, secure in the identities the happenings once attacked'.[14]

The significance of the original context noted by Danto was perhaps felt more acutely with replicas of props used in performances heavily based on audience participation or impregnated with psychological and emotional tension. One can think, for example, of the aluminium box built by VALIE EXPORT for *TAPP und TASTKINO* (TAP and TOUCH CINEMA) in 1968 and meant to be worn on her chest (the front side was made of foam, blocking the view of the artist's body but allowing people to pass their hands through slits and touch her bare breasts), or the objects placed on a table in Marina Abramović's *Rhythm 0* (1974), among them weapons and potentially harmful utensils that the audience could use freely on the artist. The material components of both performances were remade for *Out of Actions*. Audience participation, physical contact with the performer, and unpredictability and risk were crucial elements of these works, but were obviously absent from the objects evoking them, however faithful the reconstructions. In these two cases, objects were, however, not just tools to carry out actions. They were also the embodiment of conceptual propositions – the box to pass one's hands through, the objects to be used on the artist – and appeared even more so as replicas made for display.

Reconstruction was not anathema to museums' practices. This method has long been used in conservation to recreate lost or destroyed works. Jennifer Mundy has written that 'there was a heyday of the making of replicas and reconstructions in the 1960s and 1970s', although she concedes that this method 'seems to have been undertaken without too much soul-searching'.[15] In the same period, replica also became a significant part of contemporary art practice with the tendency of Conceptual Art to flirt with impermanence (for example, Sol LeWitt's *Wall Drawings*, from 1968, come into existence according to the artist's instructions for display). And this, Alex Potts writes, 'has radically shifted the ethics of replication, both making the possibility of showing replicas much less contentious, but also creating a climate where particular care has to be taken to specify the status of any replicas being shown'.[16] Atsuko Tanaka's *Electric Dress* (1956) entered the collection of Takamatsu City Museum of Art as a replica made in 1986, 30 years after its creation.

The traditional tenets of art conservation, with their focus on objects, do not seem to apply to performance, and attempts to transmit the memory of live works were not undertaken as simple conservation enterprises. As an umbrella term, conservation denotes not only the protection of a work of art in advance of future deterioration but also the idea of restoration after damage has been done. Whatever form of repair is undertaken, conservation is a specific activity 'requiring special, well-trained skills, which are different from those of the artist, the carpenter or the sculptor', as conservator Salvador Muñoz-Viñas has explained.[17] This job implies professionals and specialists, scientific protocols, established procedures and codes of ethics. Undertaken outside the realm of conservation, reconstructions of performance-related objects did not have to follow its rules.

Curatorial practices informed by a relatively relaxed attitude towards reconstruction have laid the ground for a de facto conservation of performance. Reconstructions of objects made for a performance could be considered works of conservation as their aim is to imitate lost or destroyed objects. Yet, in their method, they operate outside the framework of professional conservation practices, and they are not subject to traditional conservation rules and procedures. Conceived to meet the needs of the exhibition and feed the museum's hunger for objects to display, they are curatorial accomplices at the crossroads of the agenda of the artist and that of the curator. Born out of conversations between them, they are, quite literally, the products of DIY conservation.

The case of the exhibition *Joan Jonas: Works, 1968–1994* (Stedelijk Museum, Amsterdam, 1994) exemplifies the situation faced by artists and curators. As scholar Robin Kathleen Williams has written, the 'question of *how*, exactly, to show [Jonas's] performance works remained open-ended'[18] in the preparation of the exhibition until the artist and the curator, Dorine Mignot, opted for the construction of five installations evoking past performances. At the Walker Art Center, the curator Siri Engberg has spoken about her involvement in the creation of an installation comprising videos, recorded sounds and objects such as a table, a fan, a chair and a wig, all based on Meredith Monk's performance *16 Millimeter Earrings* (1966), for the exhibition *Art Performs Life: Merce Cunningham / Meredith Monk / Bill T. Jones* in 1998.[19] The conception and specific technicalities, meant to be the prerogative and responsibility of professional conservators, were devolved to the artist and the curator, who turned impromptu conservators.

Material and Conceptual Authenticity

The ad hoc distribution of roles in the fabrication of reconstructions in the 1980s and 1990s was not without side effects. When the setting of Marina Abramović's *Rhythm 0* was reconstituted at *Out of Actions* in 1998, Studio Morra in Naples, Italy, where the performance had been presented in 1974, was 'extremely angry about this presentation, claiming that they had the original objects',[20] according to the artist. How troubled the waters of reconstruction had become was laid bare in 1989 when Carl Andre and Donald Judd disavowed replicas of sculptures, part of the Panza Collection, which were remade without their consent for an exhibition at the Ace Gallery in Los Angeles. As Rosalind Krauss observed, 'the fact that the group countenancing these refabrications is made up of the works' owners (both private collectors and museums) – that is, the group normally thought to have most interest in specifically protecting the status of their property *as* original – indicates how inverted this situation is'.[21]

Loose instructions, improvisation, unpredictable outcomes, audience participation and multiple presentations are among the factors that make the notion of originality crumble in regard to performance. Despite this, a sense of the original can persist when a performance is repeated, especially if a new iteration takes place a long time after the first presentation or if it sticks as closely as possible to it. Another factor contributing to the perception of an original in performance lies in '"historical" executions' which are 'auratized', as Sven Lütticken writes, explaining that, 'Written accounts and especially black-and-white photographs created a mystique around such iterations'.[22] All this came into play when Saburo Murakami walked through and pierced seven large sheets of paper mounted on frames at the opening of *Hors limites* in 1994 (fig.9). The event was strikingly similar, in its formal features, to the action he had performed 38 years earlier at the second Gutai exhibition, in Tokyo in 1956 (this action was then photographed by Kiyoji Otsuji). By contrast, Allan Kaprow, who witnessed Murakami's performance at *Hors limites*, had early on in his career resolutely kept at bay the possibility of new presentations of his live works being imitations of their first occurrence. It was this stance that led him to impose precise conditions on the new presentation of *18 Happenings*

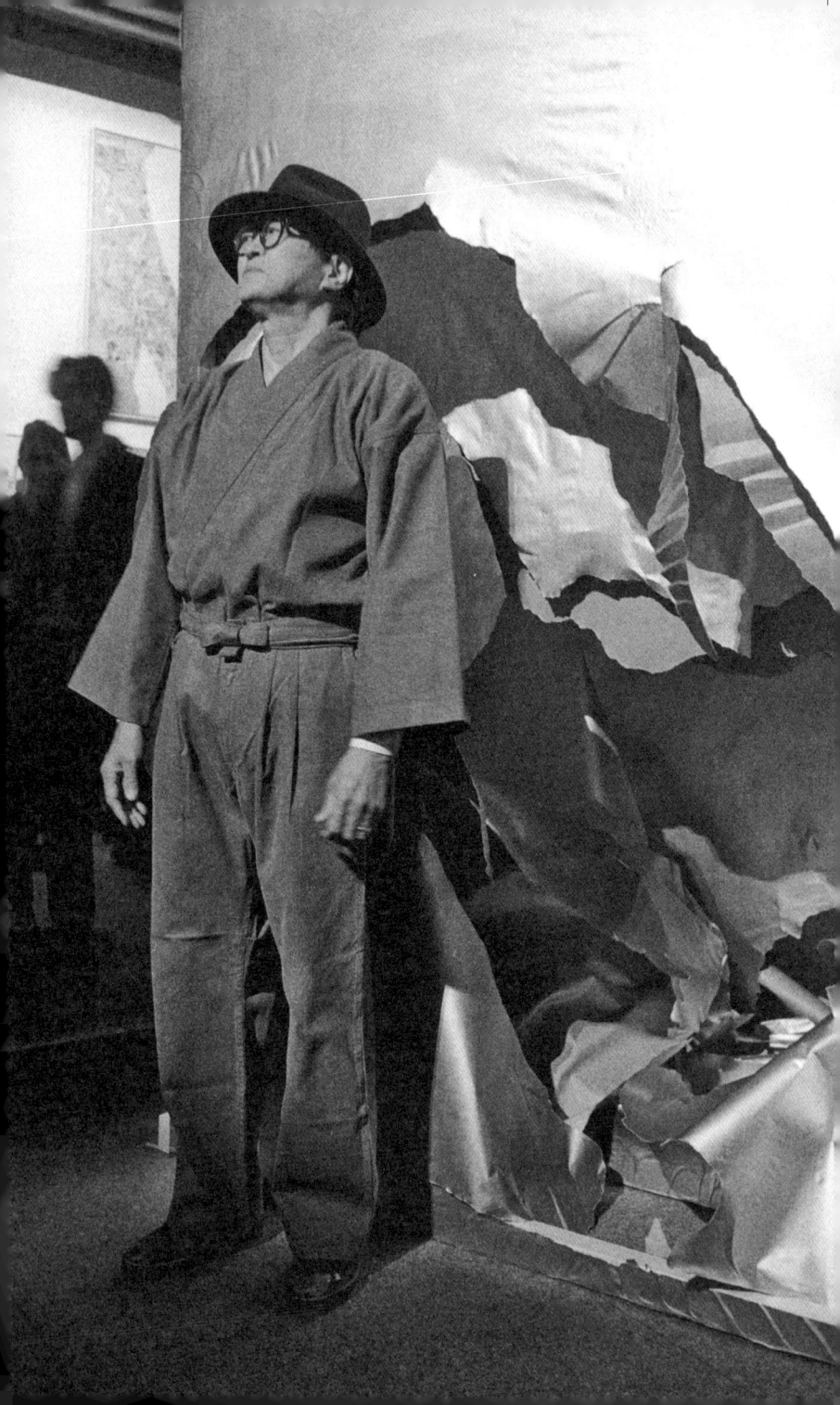

in 6 Parts at *Out of Actions*, dismissing the idea of an original and, with it, that of its replication.

Murakami and Kaprow's positions correspond to two poles in conservation culture. Whereas traditional conservation aims at maintaining the original materiality and appearance of an object through interventions as minimal and neutral as possible, the conservation of objects that have substantially deteriorated became less focused on the physical features of a work and instead depended on 'the subject's ability to derive a message from the object', as Salvador Muñoz-Viñas has written, concluding that: 'Objectivism in conservation is thus replaced by certain forms of subjectivism'.[23] This interpretative approach privileged an engagement with the artist's intent, or what can be considered the conceptual authenticity of the work.

The reconstruction of performance material swayed to and fro between objective and subjective models of conservation. Making their way through patchy documentation, hard facts, exhibition constraints and material resources and limitations, reconstructions were guided by hands-on approaches whereby painstakingly faithful imitation shades into unashamedly subjective interpretation. Essential to DIY conservation was the elasticity of its methods and procedures, which allowed room for interpretation and concessions that suited temporary display. Not uncommon at the time, DIY conservation could also be applied to sculpture, for example when Art & Language's large installation of filing cabinets *Index 01* (1972) was remade in 1989 for *L'Art Conceptuel, une perspective* (Conceptual Art, A Perspective), at the Musée d'art moderne de la Ville de Paris, as a compromise between the artists' request for a faithful copy and the museum's preference for a modified version adapted to the gallery.[24]

In the context of the growing legitimacy of conservation as a *creative* activity (not merely in a technical sense, but also in an artistic sense)',[25] as Muñoz-Viñas writes, the reconstruction,

Opposite: Fig.9   Saburo Murakami at the exhibition *Hors limites: L'art et la vie 1952–1994* (Off Limits: Art and Life, 1952–1994), Centre Pompidou, Paris, 1994

Overleaf: Fig.10   Ben Vautier, *Ben's Window*, 1962/93, mixed media, 318.75 × 454 × 274.3 cm (125 ½ × 178 ½ × 108 in.)

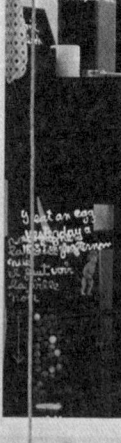
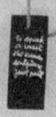

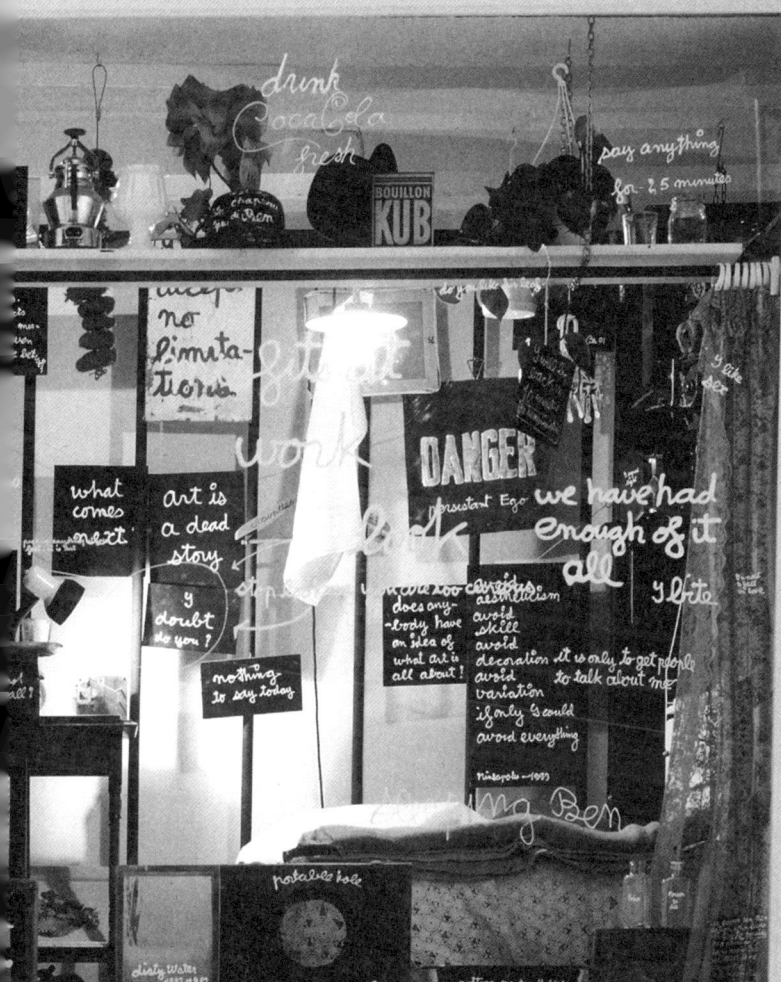

at *In the Spirit of Fluxus*, of the vitrine of Gallery One in London where Ben Vautier had taken up residence for a few days in 1962 epitomises the equilibrium reached between the restitution of original material features and a bet on conceptual authenticity. Primarily guided by the replication of the material occurrence of the performance, the new installation, entitled *Ben's Window* (fig.10), reconstituted the hotchpotch of objects that had been necessary for Vautier to live there, as well as the facade and door of the gallery. In 1962, however, the interior had evolved constantly during its domestic use by the artist, rendering an imitation impossible. At *In the Spirit of Fluxus*, different stages of the environment were amalgamated in the new work, forming a composite that stood for the work's entire existence.

Ben's Window did not just imitate and replicate, it claimed to encapsulate the 'spirit' of the work (to borrow from the title of the exhibition) and delivered its own interpretation of the material and conceptual integrity of the performance. It also bore the marks of material restrictions as it was remade as a compressed version of the original space of Gallery One, its depth considerably reduced. This shrinking of the depth was not dissimilar from that presiding over the remaking of Arman's *Le Plein* (Full Up), an enormous heap of rubbish piled up behind the window of a Parisian gallery in 1960 and reproduced, scaled-down, at *Hors limites*. Nor was it fundamentally different from the partially tilted wooden floor of Vito Acconci's *Seedbed* (1972), which was built, in a shorter version, at his 1980 retrospective in Chicago, to resemble the ramp installed at the Sonnabend Gallery in New York in 1972, under which the artist laid down, masturbated and narrated his fantasies aloud. In their new embodiment, these reconstructions were not meant to be used, or entered or stepped on. The flattening operation suggested a frontal presentation that indicated tailor-made fitting to the gallery. These alterations encapsulated the ambiguity of their status. Conceived from a perspective of conservation in the context of an exhibition, reconstructions blurred the imperatives of display of the museum and its duty of care.

RE-ENACTMENTS

Live History Repeated

'[W]here does the original reside in performance?', curator Alex Farquharson asked in 2003. 'Are film and photographic documentation, relics and physical residue [as in *Out of Actions*] the most authentic connection we now have with the original event, or do these fragments pale next to a faithful re-enactment?'[26] His reflection signalled an evolution of the debate on the afterlife of performance, whose focus was moving from the object towards live works. Farquharson pondered these questions in the light of recent live programmes in public galleries and museums, among them *Tate & Egg Live* (launched in 2003) and other events presented at the recently inaugurated Tate Modern in London. This phenomenon, he asserted, was 'founded on the assumption that the liveliness of a gallery programme is now in direct proportion to the degree of live art input'.[27]

This increased visibility of live art in the museum happened against the background of a segment of art institutions affirming their identity against large and long-established museums. Jens Hoffmann wrote in 2007, 'Intellectually and politically ambitious exhibitions have been moved out of the major museums and are more at home in smaller institutions', arguing that 'museums have become the arena for blockbuster exhibitions'.[28] As for Claire Bishop, she observed a drive for experimentation in (often medium-size) institutions run in the ethos of New Institutionalism, rather than in large museums. She wrote in 2004 that there was a 'visible tendency among European art venues to reconceptualize the "white cube" model of displaying contemporary art as a studio or experimental "laboratory"'.[29] Bishop saw this phenomenon as a response to a type of art practice developed in the 1990s which was 'open-ended, interactive, and resistant to closure, often appearing to be "work-in-progress" rather than a completed object'.[30] This 'laboratory paradigm' did not necessarily involve performance. But in the context of an experimental edge being sharpened in opposition to museum 'blockbusters' and their presumed focus on fixed objects, the display of live works appeared as a particularly fertile ground for innovation.

For Farquharson, the most 'curatorially ambitious' of the events putting forward 'liveness' was *A Short History of Performance – Part One*, mounted at the Whitechapel Gallery in London in 2002. Consisting exclusively of re-enactments of historical performances from the 1960s and 1970s, the exhibition's declared aim was to privilege 'the live event – to once again bring the work in direct relation to an audience'.[31] Live works were presented each evening for seven consecutive days in the main gallery, in an exhibition-cum-festival that ostensibly shunned the display of reconstructions, documents or relics. Framed as a fresh contribution to the reconsideration of historical performance, *A Short History of Performance* unmistakably promoted itself as an alternative to the object-based approach that had become a feature of exhibitions in the 1990s.

In a sign of the Whitechapel Gallery's awareness of the novelty, peculiarity and ambition of *A Short History of Performance*, and perhaps also of the potential contentiousness of the repetition of historical performance, a debate was organised before the opening. In this discussion, Anna Dezeuze reported, 'devoted fans of performance art expressed their concern that a re-enactment would take away the authenticity, spontaneity and radicalism of performance art in the 60s'.[32] The discernible nervousness about the enterprise was shared by Carolee Schneemann. A few days before a new iteration of her work *Meat Joy* (1964) was presented by a group of young performers as well as herself, she confided, 'It might be a serious disaster, it might be vaguely interesting, or it might reconstitute some of the motivating energies' of the work.[33]

Most of the re-enactments shown at *A Short History of Performance* were cautiously conservative in their renditions of works which had been first presented several decades earlier. As Bruce McLean assumed various positions in studied balance

PERFORMANCE IN THE MUSEUM

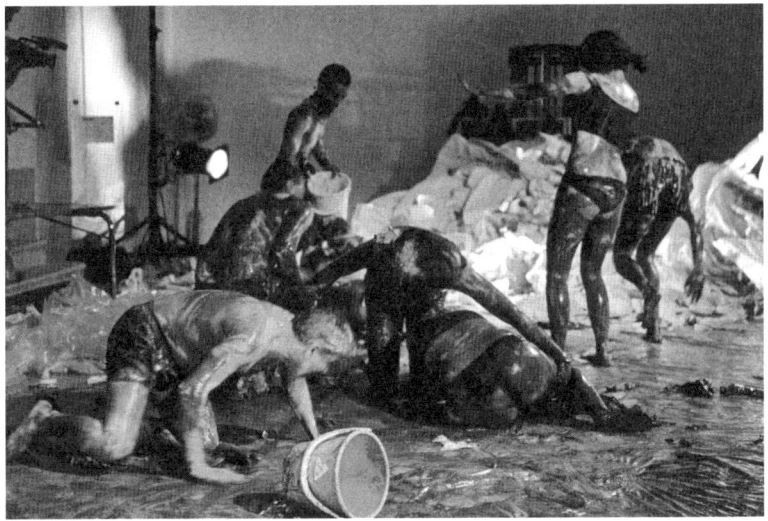

Fig.11   Carolee Schneemann, *Meat Joy*, 2002,
installation shot, Whitechapel Gallery, London

using three plinths of different heights (*Pose Work for Plinths*,
1970) and Stuart Brisley dragged his body in shallow pools
filled with chalk, flour or paint (*Beneath Dignity*, 1977),
both adhered closely to the initial presentations of their work.
Schneemann too imitated the 1960s versions of *Meat Joy*,
although she took the liberty to cast herself in a different role,
not appearing among the group of semi-naked performers
moving and rolling on the floor but instead throwing chickens
and sausages onto them (fig.11).

The risk of faithfully replicating the previous actions
was that it made all too evident the passing of time. In the
press, Sarah Whitfield regretted the dance-like movements
of McLean's early days performances, judging that 'He may
still possess this astonishing grace but it was no longer
in evidence'.[34] As for Rachel Withers, she deemed that *Meat
Joy* was re-enacted by 'a group of evidently sincere but mostly
shy and physically unconfident volunteers'.[35] What was called
into question in such imitations was the supposed immutability
of the works, as if they could be repeated unchanged, ignoring

the passage of time. First iterations were used as a template, a model to conform to, rather than an idea to interpret and a framework to play with.

It was exactly this caveat that Jens Hoffmann seemed keen to avoid when he invited young artists to make their own versions of historical performances at Kunst-Werke in Berlin in 2001. The curator explained, 'I didn't ask the artists to reenact works from the '60s and '70s – I could have used actors – but to work with original pieces in a creative manner'.[36] The result was *A Little Bit of History Repeated*, held over two evenings and, manifestly taking a stand against dominant museum practices, consisting entirely of live works. Reinforcing further the distinctness of its curatorial proposition, the exhibition not only acknowledged the time interval but even staged the generation gap. Encouraged to take possession of the history of performance, artists grafted their practice onto an artistic lineage and simultaneously affirmed their own identity. Tracey Rose covered her skin with marks of love bites in reference to Vito Acconci biting himself in *Trademarks* (1970), Michael Elmgreen and Ingar Dragset drew on Terry Fox's six-hour performance *Levitation* (1970) by locking the audience outside Kunst-Werke for 20 minutes at the time when the event was supposed to begin, and Tino Sehgal gave an interpretation of John Baldessari's video *I Am Making Art* (1971) by performing a short history of dance. 'I wanted to become a museum myself', Sehgal declared after the event.[37]

Also at *A Little Bit of History Repeated*, Laura Lima reworked Yoko Ono's *Cut Piece* (1964) by delegating the role of the performer to a goat wearing a dress, ensuring that the question of the passivity of the performer was obvious by using a domesticated ruminant. *Cut Piece* was also reinterpreted by Mai Ueda at *Re-Enact* (Mediamatic, Amsterdam, 2004) and by Ming-Yuen S. Ma in the context of the exhibition *Draw a Line and Follow It* at Los Angeles Contemporary Exhibitions in 2006. These artists belonged to a generation for whom historical performance was always historically distant and, for them, re-enactment inevitably entailed a conscious act

of appropriation. By contrast, when Ono herself redid
Cut Piece at the Théâtre du Ranelagh in Paris in 2003, she sat
stoically in a fashion very similar to the original setting, while
also claimed this version was a comment on recent events.
'In France, the organizers placed a full page newspaper by
Ono who described her intervention as a response to political
changes in the wake of 9/11', Jennifer Allen explained. In her
analysis, 'It seems that Ono hoped that her performance would
reenact the peace movement of the sixties on a global scale.
In this case, the reenactment searched for a lost totality,
not in the performance, but in an entire generation.'[38]

The Conservation of Unfixed Artworks

The possibility of reactivating historical works sparked a debate
about the conservation of performance. An unformulated
matter when reconstructions and replicas were watchwords
in exhibition-making in the 1990s, the very idea of conserving
performance became explicitly articulated when a range
of museum professionals, among them conservators, started
to weigh in. At the frontline of the challenges posed by
immaterial works, museums realised they had a vested interest
in framing this discussion within the rigorous parameters
of professional and scientific methods of care. Around
2000, performance was considered from the perspective
of conservation as part of a broader group of works which
did not fit the category of fixed objects.

Under the aegis of the Guggenheim Museum in New York,
the conservation research group Variable Media Initiative
emerged in 1999 to consider possible conservation strategies
for works that were ephemeral or whose configuration
was changeable. Introducing this project at the conference
Preserving the Immaterial: A Conference on Variable Media
at the Guggenheim Museum in 2001, artist, scholar and curator
Jon Ippolito explained that the idea was to think beyond
traditional medium categories and 'to talk about the artwork
as a dynamic medium. What are the behaviors of that artwork?'[39]

Central to this perspective was the ability of 'variable media' to be embodied in another medium endowed with a durable form. A speaker at the event, artist Robert Morris explained, for example, that the re-enactment of his work *Four Pieces* was staged in 1993 only for the camera. He saw Babette Mangolte's film as 'a record. And so, if the performances were ever restaged, we would be able to consult the film, and it would be a convenient way to restage them, if someone wanted to do that.'[40]

Museums started to reflect on the conservation of specific categories of artworks that were not permanently fixed – one could say non-solid artworks – for which traditional methods of conservation and technical management proved inadequate. In 2004 the consortium Matters in Media Art brought together Tate in the United Kingdom, the Museum of Modern Art in New York and the San Francisco Museum of Modern Art to ponder the care of time-based art in general. Between 2004 and 2007 the initiative Inside Installations: Preservation and Presentation of Installation Art, which involved the Museo Nacional Centro de Arte Reina Sofía in Madrid and Tate among other institutions, focused on installation through 33 case studies. In 2010 the Panza Collection Initiative was launched by the Guggenheim Museum in New York to tackle the conservation of works in its collection acquired from Giovanna and Giuseppe Panza di Biumo, essentially pieces of Minimal and Conceptual art by artists such as Robert Irwin, Donald Judd, Robert Morris and Lawrence Weiner. The terms and conditions that govern the production, ownership and display of ephemeral and variable artworks were examined in discussions taking place at the crossroads of art history and art conservation.

When in 2005 the Guggenheim Museum developed its research programme with the conference *(Re)presenting Performance*, gathered round the table were scholars and also artists, such as Janine Antoni, Tehching Hsieh, Babette Mangolte (who filmed and photographed many performances in the 1970s) and Carolee Schneemann. Scholars emerged as specialists of performance in a field once dominated by the question of the authenticity of the one-time live event. From the 1980s on, art historian Rebecca Schneider reminded the conference, '"Performance is ephemeral" became a kind of mantra for performance studies'.[41] In the 1990s reflection moved towards the question of 'experiencing performance as documentation', to borrow from an article written by Amelia Jones in 1997,[42] an evolution that set the tone of the conference. Peggy Phelan stressed that 'once the document is fixed, that which is in the document cannot be transformed by the one who looks', to which Schneider replied that 'to read a document as shutting down the live event of which it is a part is a problem'. Amelia Jones reinforced, 'to forget the liveness of that document in circulation is an ethical forgetting'.[43]

Marina Abramović: Seven Easy Pieces (2005)

The conversation happening at the Guggenheim Museum in New York during the *(Re)presenting Performance* conference took on a particular resonance as it coincided with the preparation of the exhibition *Marina Abramović: Seven Easy Pieces* at the museum, also in 2005 (fig.12). Essentially consisting of Abramović redoing 1960s and 1970s works by five other artists (to which she added two works of her own), it was opportunistically presented as an examination of 'the possibility of redoing and preserving' performance.[44] This exhibition constituted a significant push in considering re-enactment as a form of conservation of performance.

The use of documents in Abramović's appropriations became the object of particular interest as, interviewed by Nancy Spector, the artist acknowledged that her renditions were based on incomplete and fragmentary documentation. She explained, for example, that there was no recording of Vito Acconci's *Seedbed* (1972) although 'ninety percent of his work is about the voice',[45] and it was unclear to her whether VALIE EXPORT had a machine gun when she presented *Action Pants:*

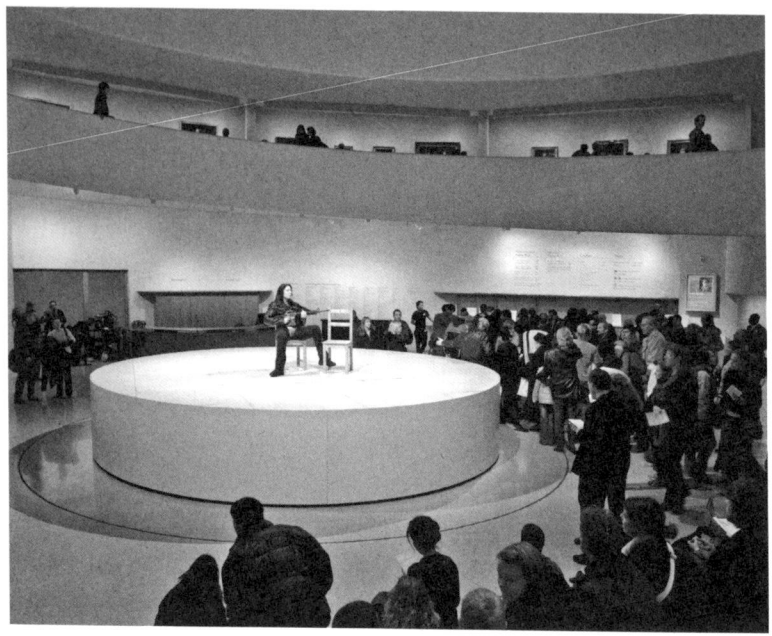

Fig.12   Marina Abramović, *Seven Easy Pieces*, 2005,
Solomon R. Guggenheim Museum, New York

Genital Panic in Munich in 1969. In addition, she was granted
permission by the Estate of Gina Pane to remake only one
part of *The Conditioning*, the first action of *Self-portrait(s)* (1973).
These limitations did not dilute the impact of the exhibition.
Every night for a whole week, in the monumental rotunda
of the museum, the artist performed live perched on a huge
platform, its curved shape echoed by the spiralling ramp
of the galleries.

It was not totally new for Abramović to put forward
her own kind of performance exhibition. In 1992, four years
after the end of her relationship with Ulay, her artistic and
life partner, she smashed principles that had hitherto guided
her art practice by recreating her past works in a stage
production. In *The Biography*, conceived in collaboration
with film and video artist Charles Atlas, she staged shorter
versions of performances and focused on key moments such

as the cutting of a star on her belly with a razor blade in *Lips of Thomas* (1975). In the absence of her former partner, slides aided the evocation of works originally performed by the duo.

In *Seven Easy Pieces* Abramović pragmatically took a wrecking ball to all re-enactment codes of the time. Weaving the patchiness of documentary sources into her own reworkings, her performances often concentrated on single moments captured in photographs. To evoke VALIE EXPORT's *Action Pants*, she sat with a machine gun, wearing trousers with an open crotch, and occasionally stood up and stared indiscriminately at audience members in a rendition that borrowed as much from the original performance, during which VALIE EXPORT confronted the audience of a cinema with a similarly cut garment, as from the photograph taken afterwards, in which she posed holding a gun. All the works of *Seven Easy Pieces* were re-enacted over seven hours, stretched to a standardised period to fit in with the extended opening hours of the museum for the show, late at night, and streamlining the week of events as one neatly packaged entity.

The inclusion of a redoing of her own piece *Lips of Thomas* in the programme emphasised Abramović's role as a protagonist in the history of performance, thus instilling an unorthodox sense of authenticity into her appropriation of works by others. For all the contradictions of its attempt to convey a sense of the radicality of historical performance in the regulated, monumental and mediatised setting of the museum, *Seven Easy Pieces* made a big splash. A live textbook on the history of performance and a solo group show of sorts, its utter uniqueness and disconcerting ethics quickly made it an unavoidable point of reference in the debate on the repetition of historical live works.

Performance Documentation

Barbara Clausen has explained that the exhibition *Wieder und Wider* [Again and Against]*: Performance Appropriated*, which she curated in 2006 with Achim Hochdörfer at

MUMOK – Museum moderner Kunst Stiftung Ludwig in Vienna, 'took its outset in the discussions sparked by Marina Abramovic's now-iconic performance series *Seven Easy Pieces*'.[46] These discussions revolved around the representation of historical performance in museums and tended to look closely at the nature of its traces. They were largely shaped by the idea of 'the performativity of performance documentation', to paraphrase Philip Auslander, who wrote in 2006 that 'the act of documenting an event as a performance is what constitutes it as such'.[47] Among exhibitions contributing to the enquiry, *Art, Lies and Videotape: Exposing Performance*, put on at Tate Liverpool in 2003, included a section headed 'Me and My Camera' dedicated to foregrounding photographers and filmmakers. One of them was Babette Mangolte, whose photographs and films of performance were often occluded by the 'real work' that is the live piece.

In a burst of interrogation, exhibitions examined the intricacy of the representation of historical performance and deliberately aimed at complicating the issue. Standing back from the assumed predominance of the live event over documentation, they flaunted their ambition to contribute critically to the debate. Exhibitions responded to one another and scheduled boosted programmes of talks, sometimes affirming entrenched curatorial and theoretical positions. A consideration of the relationship established by the viewer with the material traces of performance occupied a central place in discussions informed by recent artistic developments and scholarly research. In 1997 Amelia Jones stressed the particular subjectivity of the appreciation of performance as she wrote, referring to art of the 1960s and 1970s in relation to her own experience, 'I was thirty years old – then 1991 – when I began to study performance or body art from this explosive and important period, entirely through its documentation'.[48]

In Vienna, *Wieder und Wider: Performance Appropriated* exposed the mechanisms of the repetition of performance, almost inevitably from documentation, with live performances, sculptures, installations, lectures and debates all forming an intrinsic part of the event. Clausen had kicked off this investigation the previous year, in 2005, with *After the Act: Die (Re)Präsentation der Performancekunst* (The [Re]Presentation of Performance Art), which was also held at MUMOK and similarly included a series of talks. In this exhibition, Joan Jonas's *Organic Honey Archive* (1972–80) was emblematic of the emphasis on the role played by documentation in the '(re)presentation' of performance 'after the act'. In this installation, photographs, unedited videos, drawings, notes and posters documented no less than six iterations of *Organic Honey* over a period of eight years.

Around the same time, Sven Lütticken examined the very idea of re-enactment when he mounted an exhibition that was resolutely combative. *Life, Once More: Forms of Reenactment in Contemporary Art* (Witte de With, Rotterdam, 2005) was a declared rebuff to the growing insistence on liveness and what Lütticken saw as its fetishisation. He wrote in 2011 about this period, 'At that point, the tradition that privileged live performance over any of the performance's other media incarnations still seemed to be strong, and my exclusive focus on video, photography, slides, and language was an implicit polemic against certain theorists and artists'.[49] Also mindful of the risk of fetishising documentation, the curator put emphasis on works reflecting on their own production and utilisation of documents. Barbara Visser's contribution to the show built on her performance *Lecture with Actress* (1997). This 'lecture' was, in fact, presented by an actress who impersonated the artist, the video of which was then used to illustrate another lecture given in 2004 by a different actress who, again, impersonated the artist. The result, presented in *Life, Once More*, was the video *Lecture on Lecture with Actress* (2004), a troubling *mise-en-abîme* created by an artist who was ubiquitous yet absent. Crucially, the history of past re-enactments trailed each presentation of a new 'lecture' – another episode would be added to this series in 2007 with *Last Lecture* (fig.13).

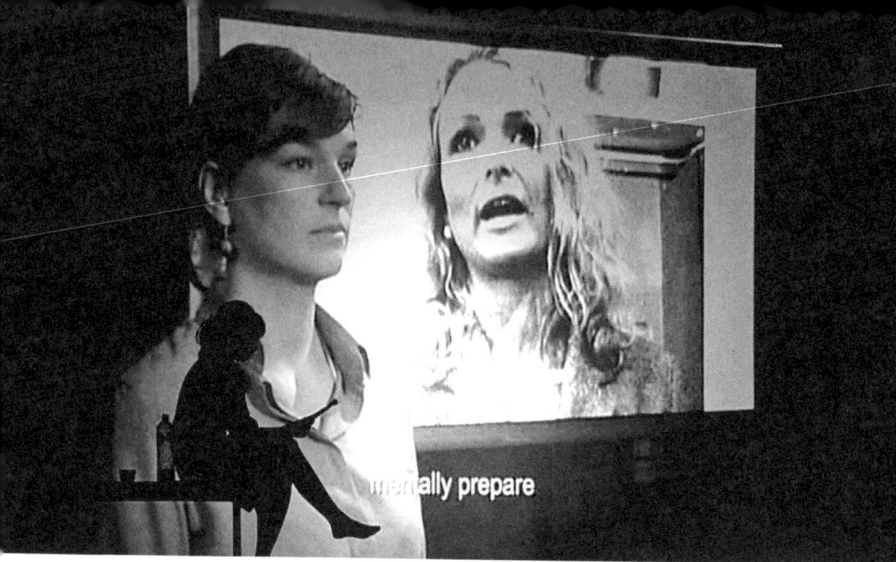

Fig.13   Barbara Visser, *Last Lecture*, 2007, performance documented on video, recorded at the exhibition *Vertaalde Werken / Translated Works, Barbara Visser 1990–2006*, Museum De Paviljoens, Almere, 2006–7

In the midst of this buzz, the Whitechapel Gallery in London delivered in 2006 the fourth and last instalment of the exhibition series *A Short History of Performance*. This instalment strikingly departed from the principle of artists performing works from their youth, which had characterised the inaugural show only four years earlier. Loosely based on the art of Allan Kaprow in the 1970s, it was firmly grounded in current discussions; its declared aim was to focus on 'the potential for a dialectical play-off between ideas of an original event and its mediation through a documentary or "reliquary" referent'.[50] Rather surprisingly, or provocatively, the exhibition featured exclusively films. At the opposite end to where the series began, *A Short History of Performance Part IV* shunned live works altogether, a sign of the direction in which the debate had moved. The echo of a 'live exhibition' might have been seen to persist nonetheless, and perhaps the feeling of a festival, as a different film (by artists such as Eija-Liisa Ahtila, Rebecca Horn, Isaac Julien, Aernout Mik and Gillian Wearing) was screened every day over the 14 days of the exhibition.

PERFORMANCE IN THE MUSEUM

At *Hors limites* in Paris in 1994, works by artists who had come to prominence in the 1950s, 1960s or 1970s resurfaced as they were replicated in the form of installations or live performance (Saburo Murakami, for example). By contrast, Allan Kaprow, always on his guard against what he saw as institutions' tendency to turn ephemeral art into fossils, created a new work for the show. His large installation, made of tyres, mattresses, barrels and fans among other objects, was conceived against the grain of reconstructions, and rather ironically it was constructed by Kaprow and his assistants in a building, located just in front of the Centre Pompidou, which was a replica of Constantin Brâncuşi's Paris studio (at the time it was closed to the public after damage was caused by flooding, before reopening, in a new version, in 1997). Shortly afterwards, the feats of replication were flaunted in the retrospective *Jackson Pollock* at the Museum of Modern Art in New York in 1998–9 with a life-size reconstruction of the painter's studio (a former barn in Long Island). Inside, photographs of Pollock at work by Hans Namuth were displayed on the walls. Valerie Casey wrote, 'Scrubbed free of the paint spills and splotched surfaces in the actual studio, the sterilized diorama at MoMA was reinterpreted and reinscribed as a different kind of sacred space, one which conformed to the ordered voice of its curatorial intermediaries'.[51]

When he died in 2006, Kaprow enjoyed a popularity that spoke not only of his influential role in the history of performance, but also of the credit given to him for his integrity vis-à-vis the afterlife of his works and his uncompromising stance on the fundamental mutability of his environments and 'activities'. His installation *Push and Pull: A Furniture Comedy for Hans Hoffman* (1963), in which visitors were invited to move objects between two rooms of contrasting appearances, served as a reference point in 2010 for the exhibition *Push and Pull* (at MUMOK and Tanzquartier Wien), a new development in the series of shows initiated by Barbara Clausen in Vienna. In this exhibition, Sarah Pierce read scripts based on documents referring to past exhibitions, such as letters and reviews (*Future Exhibitions*). These documents, Clausen noted, 'become literal markers, through which the invisible, administrative procedures the institutions maintain to anticipate and conserve "the work" as art are (re)performed'.[52] Pierce's performance, which was presented again in London in 2011 as part of a two-day event, *Tate Modern Live: Push and Pull*, exposed the cogs of re-enactment as conservation. Its self-reflexivity was that of the artist appropriating the work of another artist, as much as that of the institution hosting this appropriation.

In 2007–8 Otobong Nkanga made her own version of Kaprow's *Baggage* (1972), also titled *Baggage*. While the American artist had transported bags of sand between Rice University in Houston and a beach in Galveston, Texas, Nkanga, who is from Nigeria, shipped bags of sand from Antwerp, where she lived, to Lagos, and in return bags of Nigerian sand were sent back to Belgium. Kaprow saw his piece as one that 'mimics (or re-creates) the activity of the traveller-tourist-vacationer' and is also 'about the self – "baggage" as burden',[53] a dimension that may persist in Nkanga's interpretation. Her version also alluded to the movements of people and goods between Europe and Sub-Saharan Africa as history and art history, collective and individual memory, were interwoven in jarring patterns pointing to the consciousness of one's temporal, geographical and cultural relation to the past. This consciousness became the focal point of the work as the artist chose to narrate her performance at De Appel in Amsterdam in 2008, and then a few months later at Kunsthalle Bern. Sitting at a table and showing slides, she reported on her own appropriation in the mode of a lecture, in a setting that evoked scholarly lectures and the distanced tone that characterises them.

Chapter 3

Acquisition:
Performance Works Enter
the Museum, 2000s

In 1998 Zdenka Badovinac, in Ljubljana, curated *Body and the East: From the 1960s to the Present*, a survey of performance and Body Art in Eastern Europe, and wrote in the catalogue that 'most of the works in this exhibition were borrowed from the artists themselves, as very little can be found in the repositories of state museums'.[1] While this situation, she explained, was due to the fact that 'Eastern regimes succeeded in keeping new forms of art on the margin', the dearth of performance works in collections was, in broader geographical terms, the norm rather than the exception. The existence of gaps in collections was revealed particularly strikingly as exhibitions on performance were mounted in the 1990s. Even museums that had early on been prominently committed to the medium grasped that such commitment had rarely translated into sustained engagement with acquisitions.

In order to remedy this underrepresentation of performance in museums, which affected not only collections but also the presence of live works in exhibitions and public programmes, specific expertise was sought and developed. In 2003 Tate appointed Catherine Wood as a curator with special focus on performance, breaking with the tradition of classifying curatorial roles by regions or periods (around the same time, Tate also appointed for the first time a curator for photography and another for film). At the Museum of Modern Art in New York, a Media Department, headed by Klaus Biesenbach, was established in 2006 before 'Performance Art' was added to its title three years later. Soon afterwards, a live art department was created at the Centro de Arte Reina Sofía in Madrid.

It took the realisation that performance was the poor relation in collections for museums to take action and actively stimulate the acquisition of performance works. As museums backfilled their collections to make up for weak representation of the medium, performance sets were acquired, documents were dug up and long-lost or neglected artefacts were retrieved and purchased. At Moderna galerija in Ljubljana, Ion Grigorescu, Sanja Iveković, Jan Mlčoch and Petr Štembera entered the collection via a number of photographs and videos. As the idea took hold that performance was collectable in a wider array of forms than previously assumed, a remarkable development of acquisition strategies after 2000 gave rise to the accession of live works. Although this phenomenon represents a minute fraction of acquisitions overall, or even of museums engaging in this type of operation, it gives a glimpse of the potential of this uncharted territory.

Some performances leave barely anything material behind them, others prompt things to be produced or used during the presentation of the work, others are referenced in objects made afterwards, and all can be documented in a variety of ways. The acquisition of these works, whether as objects, documents or a live piece, is likely to trigger the process of identifying what, exactly, is acquired. This process is akin to a formalisation of the work, of its components and its status, characterising the work retroactively.

OBJECTS AND DOCUMENTS

Embroidery, Scaffolding and Gold Fillings

As a student at the University of Iowa in the 1970s, Ana Mendieta was taught that 'the process of making work – much of which consisted in ephemeral performance – involved three stages: conception, realisation and documentation'.[2] For this generation of artists, it was increasingly common to conceive performance with its material traces in mind. Amelia Jones has written, for example, that Chris Burden 'produced himself for posterity through the careful staging of each performance and its recording through photography and film'.[3] In 2006 Philip Auslander looked into the work of Vito Acconci to demonstrate that a 'performance is always at one level raw material for documentation, the final product through which it will be circulated and with which it will inevitably become identified'.[4] In Acconci's *12 Pictures*, but also *Blinks* and *Hands Up/Hands Down*, all from 1969, taking photographs was part of the works, resulting in the production of prints, which in turn provided material that could be integrated into panels and other objects, the number of which is not limited. More generally, Acconci's performances, and not just the ones involving a camera, are well documented in photographs, some of them combined with notes, sketches or maps. When these elements are arranged in multiple combinations, a single performance, such as *Following Piece* (1969), can take a variety of material forms across a number of different works.

Beyond the case of Acconci's prolific material production, performance has a history of putting in circulation works stemming from live actions. Generally speaking, however, works made out of performance have not much spilled into the market, and they have rarely sparked commercial buzz. René Block, who ran a gallery in Berlin from 1964 to 1979, has said of Joseph Beuys and Wolf Vostell that even as mature artists, 'hardly anyone was taking notice of their work back then. This made them equal to the artists of the young generation from the point of commerce.'[5] The prosaic reality of this situation was evoked by David Hammons when he stood among street sellers in Cooper Square, New York, to sell snowballs (*Bliz-aard Ball Sale*, 1983): he performed the very act of selling the ephemeral. The commercial sector only slowly woke up to the potential of performance-related objects, although gallerist Sean Kelly remembers that from the 1980s on, 'to no small extent we [art dealers] determined the way things would be formally presented and sold'[6] – a push also observed with videos sold in sophisticated containers as artist-signed editions.

As artistic and commercial practices have evolved, the presence in the market and in museum collections of performance, despite its ephemerality and stamp of unmarketability, has not been as scarce as it may seem at first glance. RoseLee Goldberg states that performance collections 'already exist inside museum collections, only by another name. They are hiding in plain sight in contemporary art galleries and scattered across departments within museums, from the library to the photography, drawing, and video and film collections.'[7] A boost in acquisitions was particularly noticeable as large museum exhibitions were mounted in the 1990s, for example when the Van Abbemuseum in Eindhoven acquired 20 videos of performances by Marina Abramović and Ulay in 1997, the year it held the exhibition *Ulay/Abramović: Video Installations 1976–1988*.

Making works with remnants of a performance, or with documents, or by combining remnants and documents together, has been a rather common practice among artists of performance. While this type of operation can be undertaken immediately after the live event, or even organised beforehand (as was often the case with Gina Pane, for example), it can also be an afterthought in artists for whom undertaking the material life of their work was not initially a priority. Wei Guangqing staged various enactments of the act of killing himself in 1988, but only used photographs of his *Suicide Project* to create a three-panel work in 2007, a piece (now part of M+ collection in Hong Kong) that also includes nooses. Similarly, Huang Yong Ping ignited explosives attached to his trousers in Xiamen in 1987, but waited until 1999 to place the charred garment in a box alongside a photograph of the original event (*Trousers with Firecrackers* entered the collection of the Museum of Modern Art in New York in 2018).

A younger generation of artists has notably expanded the material horizons of performance-related objects, and museums have increasingly acquired works stemming from performances in a great variety of mediums, materials, shapes and sizes. Maja Bajević's *Women at Work (Under Construction) in Construction* (1999), which involved the artist and female war refugees making embroideries for five days on a scaffolding erected on the facade of Umjetnička galerija Bosne i Hercegovine (the National Gallery of Bosnia and Herzegovina) in Sarajevo, entered the collection of the Musée national d'art moderne in Paris in the form of a video shown on a four-metre-high scaffolding covered with tarpaulins. Wura-Natasha Ogunji's *Beauty* (2013), in which the artist and four other women had their hair braided and entangled together while standing in a busy square in Lagos for four hours (a work alluding to Abramović and Ulay's *Relation in Time*, 1977), is evoked in an embroidered drawing – *Untitled (Three)* (2013) – in the collection of the Louisiana Museum of Modern Art in Humlebæk, near Copenhagen (fig.14). Nine black panels, covered with Gosia Wlodarczak's white drawings and forming the walls and ceiling of a box inside which the artist worked in isolation for 17 days, were acquired by the Museum of Contemporary Art Australia in Sydney in 2016 (*A Room Without a View*, 2013). As for Regina José Galindo's *Looting* (2010), it made its way into the collection of the Museum of Modern Art in New York as eight fillings made of Guatemalan gold bearing the imprints of the artist's molars.

Excavations and Bulk Acquisitions

Photographs and films of performance made for private use, rather than for commercial purposes, were not rare in the 1960s and 1970s. They might be kept by the photographers or the filmmakers themselves, by the artist or by people in the same circle. As it was not initially made for widespread circulation, this type of documentation tended to evade scrutiny. After

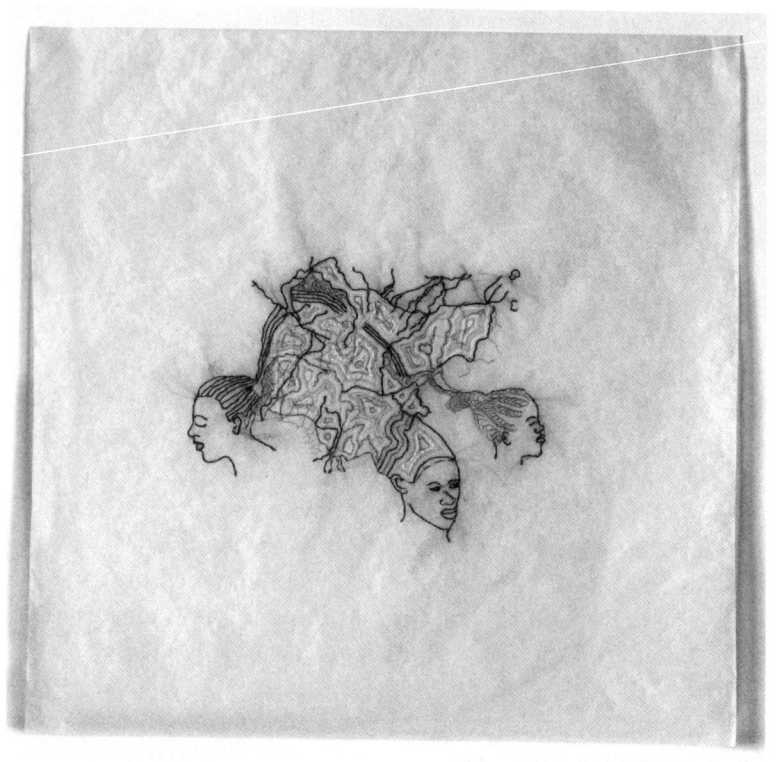

Fig.14   Wura-Natasha Ogunji, *Untitled (Three)*, 2013,
Louisiana Museum of Modern Art, thread, ink and graphite on tracing paper,
30.8 × 32 cm (12 ⅛ × 12 ½ in.)

decades of being kept as archives collecting dust or even
falling into oblivion, the excavation of long-dormant images
marked significant advances in the knowledge of historical
performance. It also opened a pathway to its presence
in museum collections.

When large numbers of documents are in the possession
of a single individual, efforts deployed by museums to get
hold of performance material can lead to acquisitions in bulk.
For example, in 2003, MUMOK in Vienna acquired more than
a thousand photographs of performances by Otto Muehl and
other Actionists, most of them taken by Ludwig Hoffenreich.

In the United States, sometime in the 1990s, Julie Martin and Billy Klüver, co-founders of the organisation Experiments in Art and Technology (E.A.T.), 'were cleaning out the basement', Martin recalls, when 'Billy discovered 60-millimeter footage of 9 Evenings [*9 Evenings: Theatre & Engineering*]',[8] a groundbreaking festival of dance, theatre and performance. The reels show works by John Cage, Yvonne Rainer, Robert Rauschenberg and Robert Whitman, among other artists, performed in 1966 in New York, in the vast space of the 69th Regiment Armory, which accommodated on this occasion telephones, radios, a large tarpaulin inflated with a fan, huge projections and even cars. Following this discovery, some of the films entered the Centre Pompidou collection between 2006 and 2008 and the Centro de Arte Reina Sofía collection in 2009.

The 200,000 photographs and negatives produced by Harry Shunk and János Kender during the 1960s were 'moldering in Shunk's hoarder-style West Village apartment' in New York[9] before they were bought by the Roy Lichtenstein Foundation in 2008 and then dispersed across different museums. Shunk and Kender documented artists' lives in Paris (they were behind the photographs of Yves Klein's *Le Saut dans le vide* [Leap into the Void] in 1960) and in New York (they took pictures of Yayoi Kusama's *Mirror Performance, New York* in 1968). When their collection was distributed between several museums, a substantial number of images relating to performance were received by the Museum of Modern Art in New York. With this mass of images, little-known events gained sudden attention, notably *Projects: Pier 18*, an outdoor exhibition held in New York in 1971 that gave ample space to performance, with works by Vito Acconci, Dan Graham, Lee Jaffe and Allen Ruppersberg, and was attended by few more than the artists themselves.

In a relatively short period of time, a very large number of items relating to live art left the domestic sphere to enter museum collections. Documents were retrieved and dusted off, photographic negatives were printed, films were transferred to video and all were organised and catalogued. Some collections had been assembled by private collectors and meticulously kept. The Fluxus collection of Gilbert and Lila Silverman – a wealth of catalogues, drawings, books, flyers, photographs, posters, notebooks, correspondence, ephemera and works which makes up the largest Fluxus collection in the world – was donated to the Museum of Modern Art in New York in 2009, and that of Marie and Milan Knížák was received by Kunsthalle Praha in Prague in 2021. All gained unprecedented public exposure as a result, as well as the care needed for their preservation.

Classifications: Art or Documentation

The acquisition of images of ephemeral works raises the question of their classification. Curator Christiane Berndes observes that when the Van Abbemuseum in Eindhoven acquired videos of Conceptual artists such as Lawrence Weiner in the 1960s and 1970s, 'the status of what we bought was unclear: Was it art? Was it documentation?'[10] In relation to performance, whether its documentation lands in the archive or in the general collection of a museum is a distinction that determines things such as the market value for purchase, the place and conditions of storage, conservation and also access, as archives are accessible to the public whereas works necessitate loan requests. As the photographs of Kender and Shunk were dispersed, the Museum of Modern Art in New York accessioned images of Kusama's *Mirror Performance, New York* (1968) and of *Projects: Pier 18* (1971) into their general collection; but the Centre Pompidou treated its lot, which included images of exhibition openings including performances, as archival material.

Whether an artefact is appreciated as a work in its own right or as supporting material providing context is a question of interpretation. In 1966 the Museum of Modern Art in New York abandoned the plan to acquire Mel Bochner's *Working*

Drawings and Other Visible Things on Paper Not Necessarily Meant to Be Viewed as Art (1966) for its research library because of the artist's inflexible request that the work, made of four identical loose-leaf notebooks on sculpture stands, be placed in the general collection.[11] The distinction between work and archival material is all the more subject to interpretation in the case of artefacts revolving around a bygone live performance. A typed letter sent by Vito Acconci to the art critic Barbara Reise as a record of *Walking Performance* (1969) is part of Tate Archive because, Jonah Westerman explains, it 'ceased to be an artwork when [Reise] treated it as correspondence, placing it with other letters and proposals for artists' projects'.[12] As informed as it can be, deciding whether an item is an artwork or the documentation of a performance is a process based on subjective reasoning, the status ascribed to an artefact being ultimately a matter of authoritative legitimacy.

Among the performance-related material entering collections, photography in particular raises the question of authorship. The numerous photographs by Ludwig Hoffenreich which were acquired by MUMOK in 2003 are generally registered under the name of the artist who conceived and presented the performance (Günter Brus and Otto Muehl, for example). Photographers tend to be recognised as artists in their own right when they develop their own artistic practice independently from documenting performance. This is the case of Kiyoji Otsuji, whose photographs of Gutai events entered the collections of the Dallas Museum of Art in 2012 and Tate in 2019 under his name, and of Minoru Hirata (mostly known for his photographs of Japanese performance, notably the Hi-Red Center), who was credited as the author of photographs of performances brought into the collections of Tate in 2012 and M+ in Hong Kong in 2015. As for Zhang Huan and Rong Rong, they share authorship of a print of *12 Square Meters*, a performance executed by the former in 1994, which is owned by the Metropolitan Museum of Art in New York.

The Unmarketability
of Live Performance

The most radical and innovative evolution in the collecting
of performance lies in a phenomenon that is numerically almost
negligible. The acquisition of live works is a breakthrough
in a landscape of performance collections fixated on objects.
Boldly pioneering, this endeavour confronts a myriad of
daunting obstacles that hitherto made it barely conceivable.
Chief of these obstructions, of course, is the sheer impracti-
cability of trading and owning works comprising living beings.
While experimenting with the commerce of the intangible
is not foreign to artistic practice, for example when Yves Klein
sold a 'zone of immaterial pictorial sensibility' at the exhibition
Vision in Motion / Motion in Vision (Hessenhuis, Antwerp, 1959)
and Yoko Ono sold her 'future mornings' in Tokyo in 1964
and in New York in 1965 (*Morning Piece*, 1964), such gestures
did little to advance the practicality of the transaction and
its implementation as a business model.

Untroubled by the downright lack of protocol for buying
and selling performance, Adrian Piper put to the test, in 1975,
the idea of the commerce of live works. She explained that she
considered making her early performances available for a fee
'for the period of time during which I was hired'.[13] In doing
so, she tentatively laid out the broad terms of a transaction
regulating the commercialisation of performance. However,
Piper conceded, 'after broaching [this idea] to a few people,
I got the general impression that no one particularly wanted
to pay for something they couldn't own, at least temporarily'.[14]
Lacking permanent materiality, performance seems therefore
to intrinsically lack the quality of an object of ownership,
a significant psychological obstacle.

The apparently unsaleable character of performance has
never completely hindered its flirtation with the market. Live
works were presented early on at art fairs, though not for sale.

With the creation of new events such as Art Basel in Miami Beach in 2002 and Frieze Art Fair in London in 2003, sparking fierce competition for attention, performance became an unavoidable feature of art fairs. It was showcased, along with other types of art at the margins of the market such as large-scale installations, in added programmes such as Art Basel's 'Art Unlimited', inaugurated in 2000, where Marina Abramović's *Self Portrait with Skeleton* was performed in 2005. The thriving relationship between this type of art and expositions did not change fundamentally the commercial situation of immaterial works. The conspicuous visibility of performance at art fairs as non-mercantile supplements only served to shed a harsher light on its stubborn unmarketability.

The implausible sense of ownership in relation to performance was overcome through the model of intellectual property. This concept, which refers to intangible possessions, enables creations of the mind to be legally acknowledged and protected. Technically, selling a live work for a lump sum consists of legally formalising a transfer of ownership. This operation grants the buyer the right to initiate the presentation of a work on demand, rather than on a one-off basis as is the case with a temporary event. This condition was key for live performance to become a possible object of commerce and ownership.

Delegating Delivery

Among the issues raised by the acquisition of live works, one is intrinsic to a medium whose main (or only) material is living beings. This difficulty seems all the more insurmountable when author and performer are conceived as a monolithic entity, binding the execution of a work to the presence of the artist. The superimposition of these two roles prevailed in historical performance, especially with works depending heavily on the ability of the artist to sustain pain or to confront danger. There were early on cases of a separation between the part of the author and that of the performer. In 1960, for example, a tuxe-doed Yves Klein assertively staged the act of deputising a work's

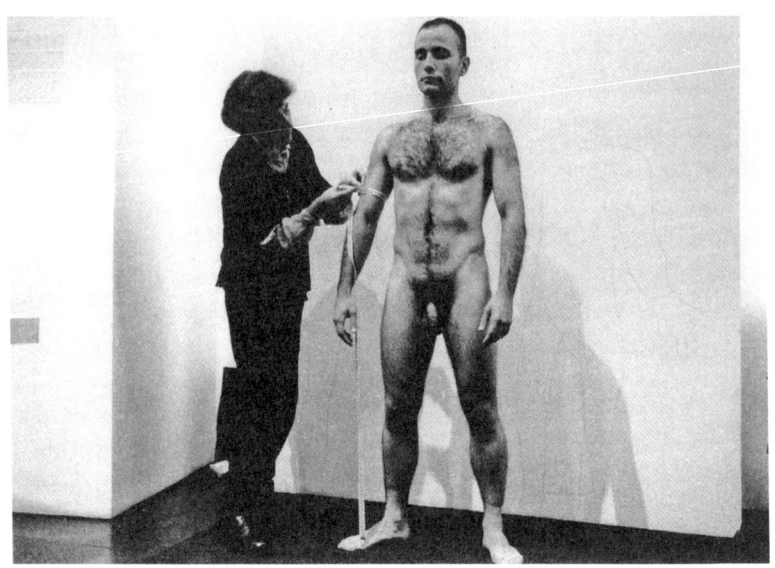

Fig.15   Esther Ferrer, *Íntimo y personal* (Private and Personal), 1967,
Collection 49 Nord 6 Est – Frac Lorraine, Metz, France

execution by directing nude models to paint a canvas with
their bodies, and in 1972 Gino De Dominicis made the transfer
of the work's execution an inherent part of *Second Possibility
of Mortality (The Universe is Motionless)* as it had to be
performed by a person with Down's Syndrome. These cases,
however, were exceptions rather than the norm, and did
not make it remotely conceivable to consider live performance
as collectable.

A more favourable terrain emerged in the 1990s when,
as Claire Bishop writes, the dissociation of the roles of artist
and performer came to dominate performance. She names
'delegated performance' works whose delivery is handed over
to performers chosen for their social, ethnic or sexual identity
or their professional expertise. This type of work, she explains,
is based on 'the act of hiring nonprofessionals or specialists
in other fields to undertake the job of being present and
performing at a particular time and a particular place on behalf
of the artist, and following his or her instructions'.[15]

In 1994, in Cologne, James Lee Byars performed *The Perfect Smile*, which revolved around the brief flickering of a smile, and shortly afterwards donated it as a live work to the Gesellschaft für Moderne Kunst at the Museum Ludwig in Cologne. This initiative, which resonated with the artist's fascination for the transience of life, resulted in a performance entering a collection as a live work for the first time. The museum is responsible for organising future executions of *The Perfect Smile* and, crucially, it can be staged without the artist present.

Relying on the employment of performers rather than the availability (and willingness) of the artist, delegated performance thoroughly changed the parameters of supply and demand for the presentation of live works. Most importantly, artworks conceived as delegated performance from the outset lend themselves more naturally to enter collections. Esther Ferrer's *Íntimo y personal* (Private and Personal, 1967, fig.15), for example, was acquired as a live piece by FRAC Lorraine, a public museum in France, in 2004. Consisting of measuring different parts of someone's or several persons' bodies, and writing the measurements down, it has been executed mostly but not exclusively by the artist since its conception. 'I plan the actions with myself in mind, but anybody can carry them out', Ferrer explains, adding, 'as long as the original idea is respected, of course'.[16]

A Big Splash in a Small Pond

The acquisition of live performance emerged as a novel type of operation and this untested enterprise was carefully watched. An important step was taken when Roman Ondak's *Good Feelings in Good Times* (2003, fig.16) became the first live work to enter Tate's collection in 2005. First presented at the Kölnischer Kunstverein in Cologne in 2003, *Good Feelings in Good Times* – a queue of people waiting without apparent reason – was made available for sale at Frieze Art Fair in 2004, where it was purchased from the artist, and entered Tate's collection the following year. At the 2005 edition of the same art fair, Tate purchased from the Jan Mot gallery in Brussels

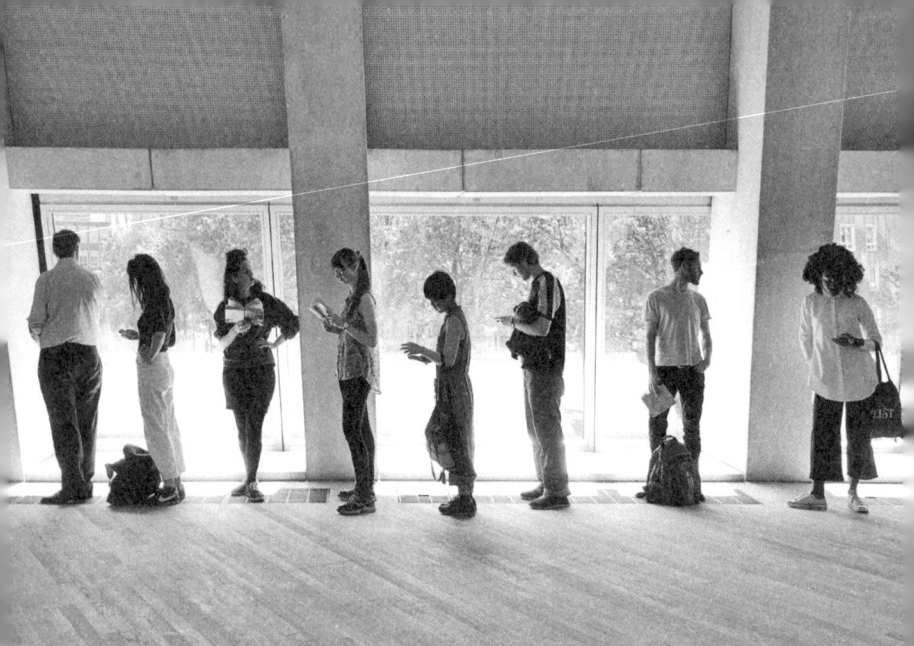

Fig.16 Roman Ondak, *Good Feelings in Good Times*, 2003,
Tate Modern, London

David Lamelas's *Time* (1970), whose participants stand
in a line 'holding' and 'passing' time, an acquisition which was
formalised in 2006; Tate also acquired a photograph of the first
enactment of the work (in France in 1970) as a discrete work.

The purchase of Tino Sehgal's *Kiss* (2003) in 2008, a work
in which a woman and a man are locked in an embrace and
kiss, marked the beginning of a swift expansion of New York's
Museum of Modern Art's collecting of live works. In 2009
the museum acquired performances including Jennifer Allora
and Guillermo Calzadilla's *Stop, Repair, Prepare: Variations
on Ode to Joy for a Prepared Piano, No.1* (2008), Michelangelo
Pistoletto's *Seventeen Less One* (2008) and Roman Ondak's
Measuring the Universe (2007). As for the Guggenheim Museum
in New York, it acquired as its first live piece Tino Sehgal's
This Progress (2006) in 2010, just after presenting the artist's
solo exhibition in a rotunda emptied of works from the
collection for the occasion.

PERFORMANCE IN THE MUSEUM

The acquisition of live performance appears as a micro-surgical revolution in museum practices. Few live works are for sale and few museums engage in this delicate operation. The vast majority of these museums only own one or a small handful of live performances. The San Francisco Museum of Modern Art acquired Ann Hamilton's *indigo blue* (1991/2007) in 2007 as a huge pile of thousands of blue items of clothing in front of which a performer sits at a table, and then Dora García's *Narrativa instantánea* (Instant Narrative, 2006–8) in 2011. Toshiki Okada's *About a Room of Memory* (2009) is based on a monologue that has to be performed next to Chiharu Shiota's gigantic sculpture *A Room of Memory* (2009), both works being owned by 21st Century Museum of Contemporary Art in Kanazawa, Japan. Roman Ondak's *Measuring the Universe*, which requires a gallery assistant to mark the height of visitors on the wall, comes in two editions (on the same principle that a photograph or a print can be issued in multiple copies); one was acquired by the Pinakothek der Moderne in Munich in 2008 and the other by the Museum of Modern Art in New York a year later.

In the small pond of artists making live works available for purchase, Tino Sehgal was championed by museums for acquisitions like no others. His 'constructed situations' (his term of choice in lieu of 'performance') are geared towards gallery settings and some are even delivered by museum staff. They entered the collection of the Museum Ludwig in Cologne and Fonds national d'art contemporain in France in 2004, the Stedelijk Museum in Amsterdam in 2005 (and again in 2017), the Van Abbemuseum in Eindhoven in 2006, Fundação de Serralves in Porto, the Art Gallery of Ontario in Toronto and the Walker Art Center in Minneapolis in 2008, the Museum of Contemporary Art in Chicago in 2009, the San Francisco Museum of Modern Art in 2010, among other institutions, and the momentum has not waned in the following years. Such success could be surprising in regard to Sehgal's idiosyncratic condition that nothing material be produced during the acquisition process (or an exhibition), not even a contract or a certificate of authenticity. As challenging and destabilising as this dematerialisation of the procedure may be, it nonetheless comes with a well-oiled set of procedures that guides the process.

RETROSPECTIVE FORMALISATIONS

The Fundamentals of Immaterial Works

A museum acquiring a live performance does not receive the work itself but information for its execution. Existing instructions, descriptions, notes, protocols, models and images are put together. Documentation is produced as artists write information down, curators undertake research and both parties take part in informal conversations or interviews, which can be recorded. The intrinsic nature of the work is defined, its constitutive features and principles are established, the terms and the conditions of its execution are specified, and this stock of information, taken holistically, carves out a mould for future presentations. In the transposition of ideas from the artist's memory and personal archives to museum files, what had remained implicit or tacit becomes explicit and intelligible. This process amounts to the formalisation of a performance.

A myriad of information is susceptible to feed an acquisition file as a result of an acquisition. Bound to a duty of care, the collecting institution must ensure that the presentation of a performance is congruent with the artist's specifications, and these specifications are multifarious. Movements in the gallery space or positions of the body, the utterance of words or sounds, the use of objects or the interaction with other people can be, among other parameters, the subject of descriptions and explanations.

At the heart of the formalisation of a performance is the nature of the actions to be undertaken and their unfolding in time. For example, the principle of Allora & Calzadilla's *Stop, Repair, Prepare*, acquired by the Museum of Modern Art in New York, lies in someone inserted in a hole pierced in the middle of a piano on wheels playing Beethoven's Symphony No.9, a piece of music often used in official ceremonies. While playing upside down and backwards, the performer slowly moves throughout the exhibition space, following a path of their choice which they have to pre-determine in advance. The acquisition file for the work also indicates that the performer should wear 'Casual clothing, preferably solid colors, not black'.[17]

Important information on a work also pertains to the performers themselves. The choice of the individuals who can execute a piece might be determined by their gender, age, ethnicity, physical features, sociological profile or technical skills, among other characteristics. The ability to play the piano is required to perform *Stop, Repair, Prepare*, while agility and suppleness are essential to perform Osías Yanov's *VI Sesión en el Parlamento* (6th Session in Parliament, 2015), part of the collection of the Museo de Arte Latinoamericano in Buenos Aires since 2016, as it involves a group of performers moving and dancing around the exhibition space and through large iron sculptures in a complex choreography. In the case of Dora García's *Proxy/Coma* (2001), which entered the collection of FRAC Lorraine in 2001, it is non-negotiable that the performer, who mingles with the visitors to the gallery, is a woman. In Pierre Huyghe's *Name Announcer* (2011), whose two editions were acquired by the Museum of Contemporary Art in Chicago and the Cleveland Museum of Art, the gender of the performer standing at the entrance of a room and announcing each visitor's name is not specified, but they must be between 25 and 65 years old, able to speak English and to stand for extended periods of time, and they are required to wear a uniform.

The association of performance with other mediums can stretch further the range of its fundamental parameters. Echoing installation and moving images, the management of the work's duration and the space of the gallery can also be the objects of detailed requirements. The performer of *Proxy/Coma*, for instance, should remain in the gallery, among visitors, during the opening time of the museum and throughout the entire exhibition; she is constantly filmed and every day a video recording of a previous day is picked at random by museum staff and screened in an adjoining room. Brennan Gerard and Ryan Kelly's *Timelining* (2014) is a complex performance in which pairs of performers talk about intimate episodes of their life from the present moment backward while walking in spiralling patterns, and when it was acquired by the Guggenheim Museum in New York in the year of its conception, issues ranging from the training of performers to their remuneration were set out in a document of nearly eighty pages. The extent of what can be considered in the formalisation of a performance is virtually without limits. The two performers painting simultaneously the walls of a room, one in black and the other in white, for Nedko Solakov's *A Life (Black and White)* (1998–ongoing), are allowed a 10-minute break every hour, but taken separately, and those queueing for Ondak's *Good Feelings in Good Times* a 20-minute break per hour when the piece is presented during an entire day (both works are part of the Tate collection).

Interpreting Artists' Specifications

Bound by a duty to care for the formal and conceptual integrity of the work, the collecting institution must ensure that decisions made for its presentation conform to the specifications formulated by the artist. This responsibility is never a matter of merely following a procedure, as specifications are inevitably subject to interpretation to various degrees. The choice of the performer, the unfolding of the course of action, the place of the audience or the material conditions of the display are among elements which may necessitate fresh decisions to be taken at each presentation. When *Good Feelings in Good Times* entered Tate's collection, Ondak specified that the queue of people should be at the entrance of a gallery, in front of a ticket desk or at other places in a gallery. He clarified, 'Positioning the queue at an unexpected – but not too obviously unexpected spot enhances its effect'.[18]

The museum is accountable for transmitting faithfully the artist's intention, and its responsibility is greatly increased when a high degree of contingency is ingrained in instructions, binding it to exercise its subjective appreciation. Tania Bruguera's *Tatlin's Whisper #5* (2008), which consists of two actual mounted police officers in uniform applying crowd control techniques to the visitors of a museum, is an example of what the artist calls 'political-timing-specific art', whose form is defined 'by the political sensibility of the time and place for which it is made'. As the Cuban artist writes, 'Form and content are interdependent, linked to the specificity of a political moment'.[19] Tate acquired *Tatlin's Whisper #5* in 2009 and its presentation is subject to an evaluation of the current political situation as the museum must ensure that it is shown 'in places where abrupt social and political events have happened either in their recent history ... or at the moment when such events are overwhelmingly presen[t] in the media'.[20] As for the Museum of Modern Art in New York, which acquired Bruguera's *Untitled (Havana, 2000)* (2000) in 2015, it must present this installation, in which four naked men stand in a dark space whose floor is covered with sugarcane, in places '(i) where the political image of the Cuban Revolution created in 1959 was idealized as a beacon for a functional utopian society, (ii) where its population have a strong emotional connection to the figure of Fidel Castro, (iii) where there is a larger concentration of Cuban population'.[21]

The Van Abbemuseum in Eindhoven bound itself to no less subjective assessment in acquiring *Positions* (2010), by the Tel-Aviv-based group Public Movement. In this work, the performers, members of Public Movement or other people trained for the occasion, are in the public space and respond to calls made through a megaphone by dividing into two groups corresponding to categories such as socialism / capitalism, gay / straight, etc. In acquiring this work, the Van Abbemuseum committed to update it to reflect the evolution of the political situation. In the same way that performers can be required to improvise or take initiatives within certain parameters,

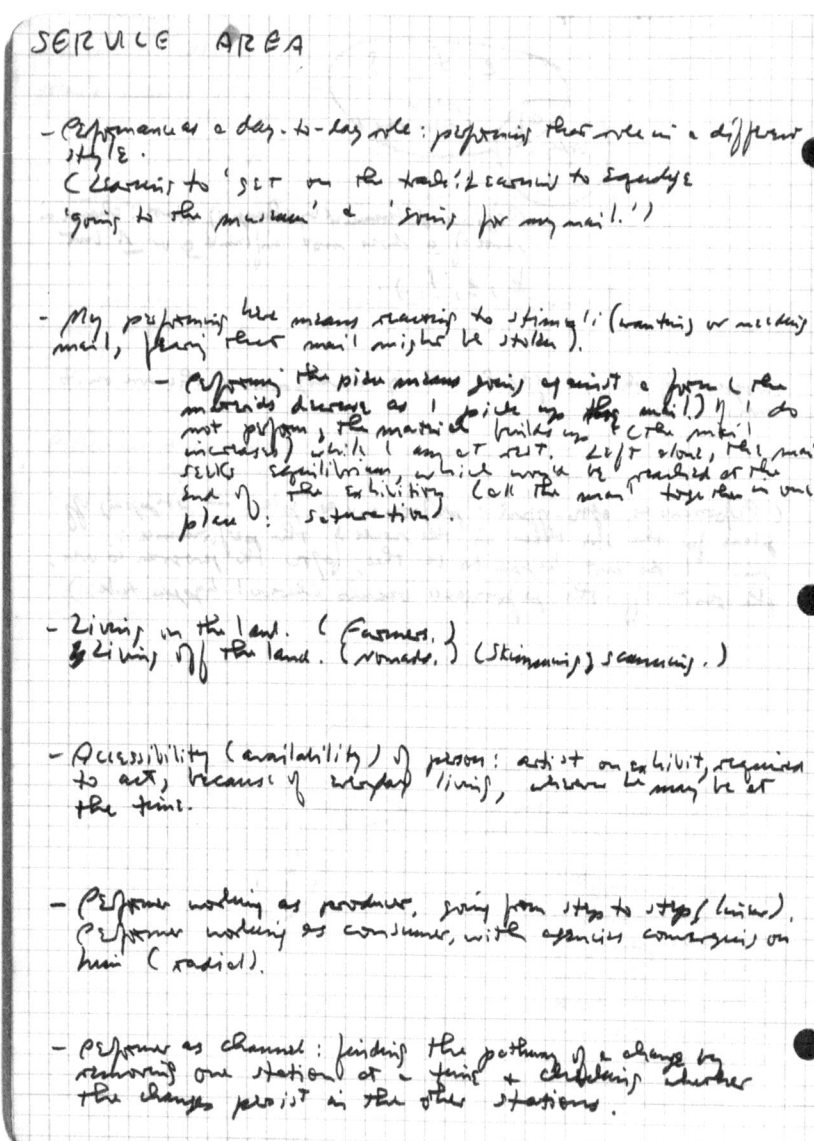

Fig.17   Vito Acconci, *Notebooks, No.2*, dated Fall 1970,
The Museum of Modern Art Archives, New York,
27.8 × 21.8 cm (10 15/16 × 8 9/16 in.)

submitting the conditions for the presentation of a performance
to such complex evaluations and interpretations casts
the collecting institution in the role of a very active agent
of the actualisation of the work.

Notations: Between Description and Instructions

What is materially taken into possession through the acquisition
of a live performance is a set of documents, whether texts,
images or sound recordings. These documents indicate how
the work should be executed, and in this respect, performance
could be aligned with what Nelson Goodman calls allographic
works. In music, for example, 'the composer's work is done
when he has written the score, even though the [musical]
performances are the end-products'.[22] The manifestation of
this type of work is based on systems of notations potentially
allowing executions ad infinitum.

There is no standard or specific system of notation for
performance. However, well before the acquisition of live
works was considered, there was a pattern of putting the
rules of action of works down on paper, thereby initiating
their formalisation. In the 1960s Fluxus embraced John Cage's
ideas of 'scores' as written instructions and published them
in books and on countless cards, packaged in specially designed
boxes, for example George Brecht's *Water Yam* (1963). The result
of the exposure of these scripts is that they were perceived less
as supplements to performance than as an intrinsic part of it.
The essential role played by language in Fluxus performance
left the door open to a potentially indefinite number of presentations, a key aspect of the formalisation of performance
operated in the 2000s in the context of acquisitions.

In 1970 Vito Acconci took brief notes about his work *Service
Area* in a notebook, describing the performance as 'a day-to-day
role', mentioning his fear that the 'mail might be stolen' and
pondering the fact that when he is at rest, the mail, 'left
alone', piles up and 'seeks equilibrium' (fig.17). In the wake

of Conceptual Art, statements formulating the chief principle of works started to become more public, and to trail performances like lexical appendices. They were printed and included in Chris Burden's 'relics' along with objects used during his actions. They nest in the title of Lotty Rosenfeld's *Una milla de cruces sobre el pavimento* (A Mile of Crosses on the Pavement, 1979), which precisely consists of crosses traced on the pavement over a mile. They comprise the bulk of the text of the book *Marina Abramović Ulay / Ulay Marina Abramović 30 November / 30 November* in 1979 (the page on *Breathing out – Breathing in* reads, 'We are kneeling face to face. / Our noses are closed with filtertips. / In our mouths are capsule-microphones. / We are pressing our mouths together').[23] These texts accompanying live works sit ambiguously between instructions and descriptions.

The various documents gathered when a performance enters a collection can pre-date the presentation of the work, or be written in its aftermath and provide information on past iterations. Both are used as a model and guidance for future executions. This dual status of documentation is manifest in works by Marie Cool and Fabio Balducci. Based on simple gestures, their performances involve the manipulation of stationery such as pencils, sheets of paper, rulers, adhesive tape or a desk; they are often delivered to an audience, and sometimes just for the camera. When FRAC Lorraine, the Museum of Modern Art in New York, the Musée d'Art Moderne Grand-Duc Jean in Luxembourg, the Musée national d'art moderne in Paris and Arter in Istanbul acquired works by Cool and Balducci between 2011 and 2013, they all received videos of performances. Works in their own right, these videos could also be used as models for future presentations, and they may be accompanied by instructions as part of the acquisition. Objects may be acquired too; for example, the Paris museum owns not only two videos but cotton thread, a mirror and a table as part of *Sans titre (fil de coton, miroir, table)* (Untitled [Cotton Thread, Mirror, Table], 2007). While the material brought into collections can be used for future displays, a tight

PERFORMANCE IN THE MUSEUM

characterisation of the works is scrupulously avoided by Cool and Balducci. Instructions and information provided are deliberately succinct, the videos are very short (a couple of minutes) and usually silent. All this works towards making the engagement of the artists in future presentations more indispensable, a situation reinforced by the fact that Cool is the sole performer of their works.

Not all performance works are suitable to enter collections, particularly if the performer is supposed to be the artist, or has always been the artist. Also, a performance is more likely to be transcribed in notes if it is based on a certain conceptual clarity, does not involve a wide range of intricate actions, and has minimal material accessories rather than a complicated setting and a whole apparatus of props. 'To describe Partial eclipse would be inappropriate',[24] Marc Camille Chaimowicz wrote as he presented his work at De Appel in Amsterdam in 1980, referring to the complexity of a 40-minute performance involving a performer walking in different fashions, smoking a cigarette and blowing the smoke so it was caught in the light of projectors; recorded music and voice; and 160 images projected on a screen. Although not intended to be repeated, *Partial Eclipse* was performed again by the artist in 1981 and 1982, and only in 2002 did Chaimowicz decide to have it performed by other people and consign notes and instructions for this purpose. This later episode proved key to the adaptability of the work to acquisition, and these detailed records, built on past presentations with the prospect of future ones in mind, were a determining factor in Tate deciding to acquire the work in 2007.

Composite Works: Ensembles

The formalisation of works on acquisition is not restricted to live action. The appetite of the museum for collecting performance-related material increasingly takes the form of objects and documents put together as ensembles. Combined retrospectively, these objects and documents claim to be an indivisible entity and constitute a work in its own right. For example, vintage photographs, negatives, slides, digital photographs, a video and catalogues relating to Lotty Rosenfeld's *Una milla de cruces sobre el pavimento* were acquired as a work by Centro de Arte Reina Sofía in Madrid in 2011. In the case of Kateřina Šedá's *There is nothing there (Game for an unlimited number of players)* (2003), a 24-hour 'game' involving residents of a small town in Czechia, it entered the collection of the Muzeum Sztuki Nowoczesnej (Museum of Modern Art) in Warsaw as a 30-minute video and a publication with maps, notes, and various documents and texts, for example on the origins of the piece ('I began spying on people') or the procedure of the performance ('I distributed to the inhabitants of Ponětovice a chart in which they were to fill in their normal Saturday routine').[25]

The formation of ensembles comes in the context of the 'exciting and daunting question' of the integration of 'non-art' objects in the institution's various collections, Elizabeth Carpenter wrote in 2014 after the acquisition by Minneapolis's Walker Art Center, in 2011, of a wide range of objects from the Merce Cunningham Dance Company, among them costumes and stage sets. The question is daunting because objects relating to performance and inconsistently sitting between the categories of artwork and archive have been a challenge to the museum. This 'formerly fraught situation is now normative', Carpenter observed, as 'opportunities to collect cross-departmentally are pursued as a matter of course'.[26]

In ensembles, acquisition provides a resolution to the statutory ambivalence and instability of documents. The distinction between the categories of archive material and work itself, and the uncertainty of the destination of performance documentation within departments, crumble in ensembles. As items are stored together as composite works, ensembles make the distinction between archive and general collection vanish. The curator Stuart Comer explains, 'For a long time, I have not seen a hierarchy between a work and the archival document, particularly in performance-related work. Is a photograph an archival index or an artwork? I would prefer to keep that rule totally indeterminate.'[27]

Formalised as such through the acquisition process, ensembles are often originally created for exhibition purposes. For example, Suzanne Lacy stamped Los Angeles maps with the word 'rape' during her performance *Three Weeks in May* in 1977, locating rapes reported daily in the city, but she only presented them with a soundtrack at the exhibition *Under the Big Black Sun: California Art 1974–81* (Museum of Contemporary Art, Los Angeles, 2011–12); both freshly associated elements were acquired as one work by the Hammer Museum in Los Angeles in 2012. Orlan's *Action ORLAN-CORPS. Le Baiser de l'artiste* (Action ORLAN-BODY. The Kiss of the Artist, 1977) was made for the exhibition *elles@centrepompidou* (Centre Pompidou, Paris, 2009–11) in collaboration with a curator, and it was acquired by the Musée national d'art moderne in Paris in 2009. It comprises a large photograph, a sound recording and documents mounted between plastic sheets, all components related to the artist's performance at the FIAC art fair in Paris in 1977, in which the artist 'sold' kisses to visitors. As exhibition display designates objects and documents to be considered together, and acquisition formalises them as parts of an indivisible whole, the artist and the curator borrow from each other's prerogatives while both encroaching upon the territory of the archivist.

Compared to Orlan's piece, the photographs, notes and press cuttings from VALIE EXPORT's personal archive forming *Vitrine TAPP und TASTKINO* (1968–9) look more contained as they are stored in a display cabinet. Made collaboratively by VALIE EXPORT and the curator Yilmaz Dziewior for the exhibition *VALIE EXPORT – Archiv* (Kunsthaus Bregenz, 2011–12), the work was acquired by the Museum Ludwig in Cologne in 2011. As its title indicates, the work entered the collection as a glass cabinet, an explicit borrowing from traditional museum furniture. While the horizontal display of the documents underlines their origin as archival material, they are institutionally framed as an artwork.

The coherence of a group of objects initially put together for an exhibition is usually made manifest by their content: typically, they all relate to one performance. But asserting the status of these objects as a whole when they cannot be contained in a display case entails delimiting a space of their own through display. This curatorial exercise is all the more necessary when the display of the elements of an ensemble necessitates ample room. *Action ORLAN-CORPS. MesuRage du Centre Georges Pompidou* (Action ORLAN-BODY. Measuring of the Georges Pompidou Centre, 1977) for example, which was made for the exhibition *elles@centrepompidou* at the Centre Pompidou and is now part of the Musée national d'art moderne collection, is formed of separate elements but expands considerably in space with a life-size cut-out of Orlan, the dress she wore when she measured the Centre Pompidou with her own body, original photographic prints and new ones, an engraved copper plaque and a number of documents.

Similarly, Mehtap Baydu's *Self Portrait: Wrapping in a Character* (2017), a performance in which the artist wore dresses collected from women of diverse backgrounds and almost suffocated under many layers of garments, was acquired by the Istanbul Museum of Modern Art; the acquisition included a video of the first presentation of the work, in Kassel in 2012, notes written by women who gave a dress to the artist for the performance, a sculpture made of the dresses used to smother the artist, and another sculpture evoking the action. The impossibility of the physical containment of these elements entails curatorial work at each presentation and exemplifies the responsibility of the curator, rather than the artist, to frame disparate elements as a single entity. As Amélie Giguère notes, unlike installations, in which 'the arrangement of various components is generally invariable and an integral part of the artist's specifications, an ensemble of documents allows variations according to the context, for example, or the space available for display'.[28]

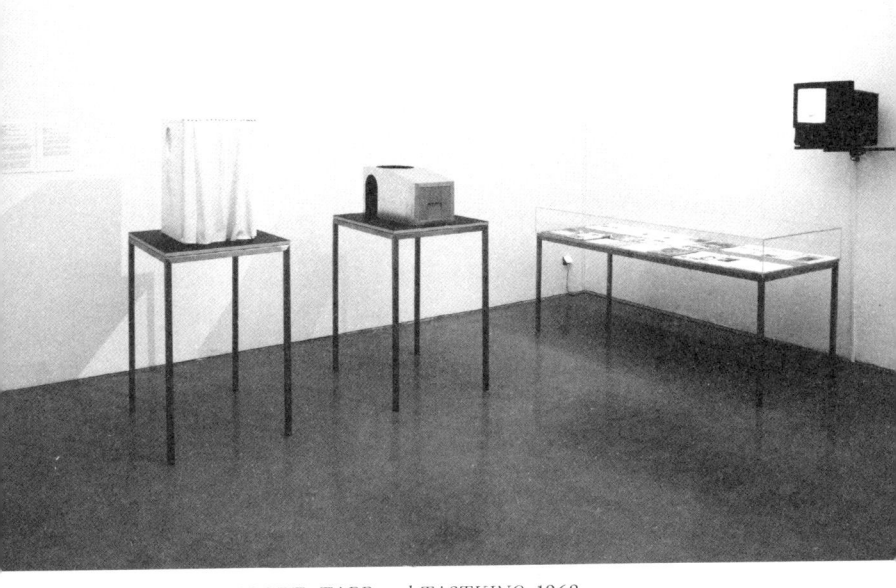

Fig.18   VALIE EXPORT, *TAPP und TASTKINO*, 1968,
Sammlung Generali Foundation, Vienna – Permanent Loan
to the Museum der Moderne Salzburg, installation view

Repositories of elements from various sources, ensembles
often summarise strategies deployed by museums to remedy the
absence of live works. The history of these manoeuvres, operated
both at exhibition and acquisition levels, appears with particular
complexity in another work from *TAPP und TASTKINO*, this
time acquired by Generali Foundation in Austria in 1999 (fig.18).
This work includes documents (photographs of the live piece,
notes by the artist, a poster and press clippings), while other
elements make it substantially distinct from the self-contained
vitrine of the Ludwig Museum. A short video documents VALIE
EXPORT presenting the work in Munich, a box attached to her
chest, and Peter Weibel, armed with a megaphone, inviting
passers-by to insert their hands into the opening in the box.
Two boxes designed to be worn in front of the chest, the bulkiest
elements of the work, complete the ensemble.

In the course of the execution of *TAPP und TASTKINO*
in the streets of Vienna and Munich in 1968 and 1969, two

boxes were made by VALIE EXPORT; the first one, in Styrofoam, was subsequently destroyed and a second one, in aluminium, was lost. The work owned by the Generali Foundation includes the metal box remade by a designer for the exhibition *Out of Actions* in Los Angeles in 1998. It also includes a replica of the first box, this one made by the artist at Generali Foundation's request to create the ensemble. These reconstructions follow in the footsteps of Ben Vautier's *Ben's Window*, reconstructed for *In the Spirit of Fluxus* in 1993 and purchased by the Walker Art Center in Minneapolis, and the 14 sheets of paper Saburo Murakami walked through at the opening of *Hors limites* in 1994, which entered the collection of Paris's Musée national d'art moderne under the title *Passage, 8 novembre 1994* (1994). The Generali Foundation ensemble, featuring a selection of documents and two different reconstructions, reveals complex strata of museum intervention.

IMMATERIAL COLLECTIONS

Alexandra Pirici and Manuel Pelmuş's *Public Collection of Modern Art* (2014, fig.19) is emblematic of the transformations that the very idea of an art collection has undergone since around 2000. The performance of the Romanian duo, both of whom have a background in dance and choreography, was acquired by the Van Abbemuseum in 2015 and, through it, evocations of paintings or sculptures by modern artists including Paul Gauguin, Edouard Manet, Pablo Picasso and Vladimir Tatlin. Conceived on the occasion of the exhibition *Confessions of the Imperfect, 1848–1989–Today*, held at the museum in 2014, this work stages the embodiment of artworks and manifestos of the 19th and 20th centuries through the actions of a group of performers miming scenes, compositions and shapes with their bodies. The selection of works and texts to be enacted was made by the two artists according to their importance in the history of art or their relevance to them personally. As the title of the performance indicates, they form a collection, albeit an immaterial one. We 'want to introduce

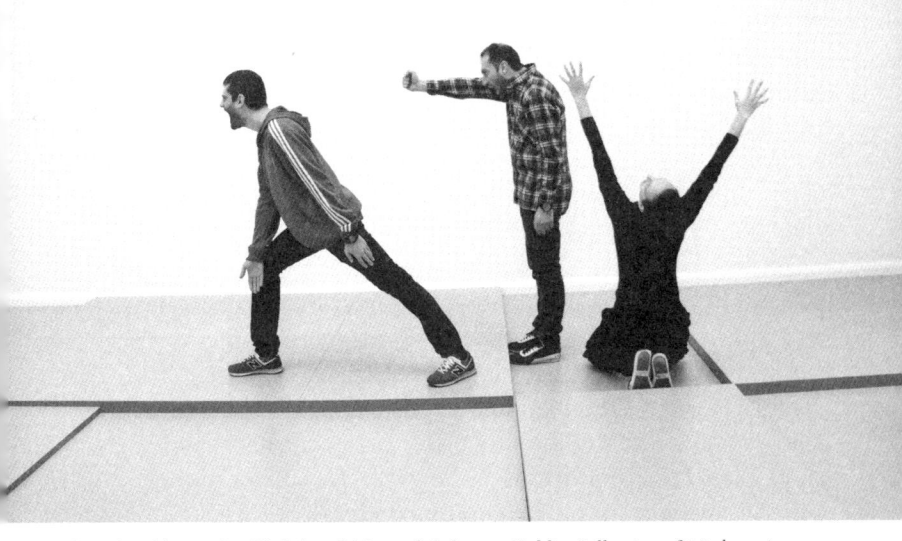

Fig.19   Alexandra Pirici and Manuel Pelmuş, *Public Collection of Modern Art*,
2014, Collection Van Abbemuseum, Eindhoven, The Netherlands.
Photo: Van Abbemuseum, Eindhoven, The Netherlands

an intangible version for a future museum', Pirici explains,
while Pelmuş adds '[to] put forward the idea of immaterial
collections containing objects that exist only when they
materialize in our actions'.[29]

In 2013 Pelmuş and Pirici had conceived another bodily
interpretation of a collection when they took over the Romanian
pavilion at the 2013 Venice Biennale and had more than
a hundred works and events mimed as their own version
of a retrospective exhibition (*An Immaterial Retrospective
of the Venice Biennale*, 2013). While they revisit the parameters
and conventions of art exhibiting and collecting through
performance, they also place their approach firmly within
an institutional context: one collection (in 2014) is 'public',
the other is a somewhat implausible 'retrospective' of the oldest
art biennial in the world. The desire to imagine live collections,
put together not by curators and museum directors but by artists,

and yet framed through the institution, is also at the heart of Hu Xiangqian's *Xiangqian's Museum* in 2010. This fictional, or perhaps simply immaterial museum comes to life as a performance where the artist describes works, which he has seen or imagined, and renders them through gestures and bodily poses.

Xiangqian's Museum and *Public Collection of Modern Art* are propositions for immaterial museum collections, but they do not invoke only performances. They refer primarily to objects and build a bridge between material and immaterial works, dismissing a perceived isolation of live performance in acquisition practices. They also indicate the many implications of an immaterial collection, which does not require storage, might expand over time and could revolutionise the very concepts of loan requests, transport, safety and costs of display. Most importantly, they also operate a rotation of roles as the artists, not museum staff, select works of their own preference without seeking approval from an acquisition committee or a museum board.

Chapter 4

Introspection:
Reflecting on Performance
in the Museum Today

Mulling over the transformation of the museum since 2000, RoseLee Goldberg predicted in 2016, 'Once thought to be too ephemeral and outside the scope of art history, performance art, and the departments now being founded to examine its history and contemporary forms, will be central to the discussion about art and culture of the future and about the institutions that will conserve, collect, and exhibit this material'.[1] Goldberg spoke in the midst of a period when bringing in performance was a major concern for the museum. The curator Catherine Wood explained in 2013 that a lot of activity around performance at Tate was driven by the question, 'How to bring the "minor" histories of film and performance into dialogue with the "major" histories of painting and sculpture, for example? How has performance been there all along but invisibly?'[2] At Tate Modern, this questioning materialised, in 2012 alone, in an exhibition (*A Bigger Splash: Painting after Performance Art*), the first live work commissioned for the Turbine Hall (Tino Sehgal's *These associations*), a symposium accompanied by performances (*Performance Year Zero: A Living History*), a programme of live performance (*The Tanks: Fifteen Weeks of Art in Action*) and a symposium (*Playing in the Shadow*) organised in relation to the inauguration of The Tanks as a space largely dedicated to live art.

The conversation developed by the museum around its relationship with performance may still be informed by a lingering feeling that its logistical and administrative structures continue to be very much crafted for objects, resulting in performance being treated as a case with special needs and requirements. The curator Stuart Comer observed in 2015:

> I think the infrastructure of every single museum is still entirely based on paintings and objects. In terms of how the registers are constructed, in terms of how art handling is organized, in terms of how exhibition schedules are organized – generally in three- and four-month blocks, rather than like a two-week festival, marketing as well, just all of the different systems in museums are still largely organized around things that are not actions or events, but things that are circulated.[3]

This opinion was summarised the same year by another curator, Jay Sanders, who asserted that in the museum, 'with performance, you still at times feel like you are running the wrong way on the conveyor belt'.[4]

The challenges posed by performance have had a deep impact on the museum across departments and areas of expertise, and they have prompted a surge of research within institutions. Symposiums have been organised, research programmes have been set up, professionals from different areas have gathered and, through these exchanges of points of view and ideas, the conversation on performance has bounced back to the role and the modus operandi of the museum itself. From the perspective of performance and in relation to its presentation, conservation and acquisition, the museum has engaged in a period of introspection.

THE RIGHTFUL MUSEUM

The Institutionalisation of the Fringes

The artist Mary Oliver recalled that in 1995 she asked the events organiser at Tate 'when they were going to open their doors to live art practice', and his reply was that 'he did not think it would be anytime soon because it was not on their agenda, but that "this decision didn't come out of any animosity"'.[5] Twenty years later, Hal Foster observed a 'sudden embrace of live events in institutions otherwise dedicated to inanimate art'.[6] As unforeseen and 'sudden' as this evolution might have been, it was firmly consolidated in the 2010s. Pablo Bronstein noted in 2019 that, 'people younger than myself will no doubt be under the false impression that performance has always existed so prolifically and been taken seriously by art institutions'.[7] It is in this context of a striking presence of live performance that museums started to scrutinise their own role in this evolution.

In 2016 Jonah Westerman introduced *Performance at Tate: Into the Space of Art* by situating this research project in the context of a question that has pervaded the relationship between performance and the museum. Writing about the possibility for a museum to collect live work, he asked:

> How would one go about doing such a thing? And if it could be done, should it be done? Such questions reflect an overarching narrative that after decades of being on the artistic fringes performance is becoming institutionalised. The carceral connotation is intended – as the story goes, the process of entering the museum entails becoming somehow disciplined and denatured by antiseptic, breathless forces of containment.[8]

In the early days of performance, museums were often perceived as too stiff to accommodate art that defied their conventional modes of operation. In the 1970s, Dominic Johnson has written, 'the anomalous body practices that artists pursued would enable them to depart from the orthodoxies that clung (and cling) to institutional and other traditions of art-making, criticism and reception'.[9] While Johnson has in mind particularly radical art practices, the museum remained a perfect tool to gauge the acceptability of inappropriate behaviour well beyond the 1970s. In 1997 Şükran Moral, wearing a provocatively revealing dress, posted herself at the entrance of a brothel in Istanbul in full view of the bemused passers-by (*Bordello*). She also hung a sign reading 'Modern Art Museum' on the door and, by doing so, not only alluded to the commercialisation of the female body in both the brothel and the museum but literally and metaphorically stood at a threshold – that of the brothel cum museum and the street, and that of the acceptable in the public space and in the art institution.

The legitimacy of the museum to present a type of art that has partly defined itself in opposition to institutional restraint is a question that resurfaced when performance became the object of institutional embrace from the 1990s onwards. Elizabeth Armstrong, who curated *In the Spirit of Fluxus* with Joan Rothfuss in 1993, remarked, 'Given that Fluxus intentionally positioned itself outside mainstream art institutions, an endeavor in which it was extremely successful, it might seem even more ironic to present Fluxus in the museum'.[10] In the catalogue of the exhibition, Andreas Huyssen, perhaps thinking of exhibitions such as the 1983 edition of the São Paulo biennial, which included a large section called 'Fluxus International & Co.', or *Ubi Fluxus ibi motus, 1990–1962*, curated by Achille Bonito Oliva during the Venice Biennale in 1990, asserted that Fluxus's new life was 'now in the museum, the archive, the academy', while reassuring readers that 'the museum today is no longer a bastion of high culture only'.[11]

Fluxus could be emblematic of the institutionalisation of anti-institutional art as it entered museum collections through a plethora of objects, for example with the acquisition of the Hanns Sohm collection by the Staatsgalerie Stuttgart in 1981.

Gilbert and Lila Silverman donated their huge Fluxus collection to the Museum of Modern Art in New York in 2009, and this accession was quickly celebrated by the museum with the exhibitions *Fluxus Preview* in 2009–10 and *Thing / Thought: Fluxus Editions, 1962–1978* in 2011–12. The acquisition of the Silverman collection, however, prompted lamentations that 'Fluxus should never find safe haven in the Museum of Modern Art – it should be forever outside', Hannah B Higgins reported. She wrote, 'The idea is absurd since the first Fluxus titled concerts were in museums in Europe, and being both for and against the professional art system, or for and against specific parts of it, has characterized Fluxus since its beginnings'.[12]

Rather than being a mere question of presence in the museum, the institutionalisation of art means its integration into an array of systems. Procedures, regulations, administration, classifications, organisational schemes, security arrangements, curatorial agendas may all affect not only the display of art but its contextualisation, interpretation and, prosaically, visual perception. Conservation techniques, for example, among them reconstructions, may unwittingly give a sense of asphyxia and the fossilisation of performance within the bell jar of the museum. Institutionalisation is made particularly blatant by the ephemerality and unfixed character inherent in performance, and it is especially identified and pointed when perceived as unnatural or illegitimate. The incompatibility of performance with the museum is not ontological, but ideological and contingent.

A stark-naked Oleg Kulik acted out his institutional unsuitability when he impersonated a dog at the beginning of his career, chaining himself up outside the Kunsthaus Zürich in 1995, barking, growling, sniffing and defecating, and then in 1996 mauling the curator of the exhibition *Interpol* in Stockholm, ending up in a police station in both episodes. By contrast, in 2003 Kulik looked exquisitely beautiful and surprisingly still as he appeared adorned in a mirror suit, brightly lit and perched on a trapeze hanging in the Turbine Hall at Tate Modern in London as part of *Live Culture*.

The title of the work, *Armadillo for Your Show* (2003), made his one-hour long performance resonate with the display of an exotic creature, raising the question of his apparent domestication.

An artwork is exposed to the peril of institutionalisation, understood in its clinical or carceral sense, if precisely conceived for a place that is not an institution. Institutionalisation is neither necessarily good nor inevitably bad or detrimental to its object. It could impose some procedures upon artworks but could also offer them various forms of protection and care. In 1970 security guards forcibly stopped Antonio Manuel from attending an exhibition opening at the Museu de Arte Moderna Rio de Janeiro naked, an act of protest against the rejection of his performance in that exhibition. Shortly afterwards, the artist made a sculpture in which a photograph showing himself during this action was encased in a box on the top of a heap of straw (*Corpobra* [Bodywork], 1970). This sculpture was acquired by a member of the jury who had unsuccessfully interceded in favour of accepting the performance in the first place, and entered the Museu de Arte Moderna in 1991 as a long-term loan, retrospectively offering lasting exposure to the unauthorised and interrupted action.

Misplaced Re-doings

The debate around the rightfulness of the museum to open its doors to performance took a new turn with the wave of re-enactments after 2000. The repetition of works from the 1960s and 1970s almost inevitably brought attention to the new context of their presentation and to differences in historical background, social circumstances, spatial setting, institutional conditions and ambience. These differences did not fail to appear strikingly pronounced, putting into question the mechanisms of such institutional embrace.

Marina Abramović's *Seven Easy Pieces* was received with the sentiment that it was like a transplant of 'the fragile seedling of a long-vanished counterculture into the hyperfortified biosphere of 21st-century art', *Art in America* reported.[13] Melanie Gilligan, for example, asserted that if Vito Acconci's *Seedbed* 'was a famously awkward piece to experience – the gallery visitor uncomfortably aware of Acconci's masturbatory pleasure below the floorboards – at the Guggenheim this piece seemed less disquieting, with any sense of taboo neutralized by the audience's and institution's general approbation'.[14] Echoing this opinion, Amelia Jones keeps in mind the lost potential of the 'surprised, confused, pressured, or otherwise destabilized gallery visitors' of the initial performances. She writes, 'Abramovic performed in small galleries in Europe for a select art world audience. Today she is at the forefront of an industrial-strength institutionalization of performance histories.'[15]

The idea of a discordance or opposition between performance and the museum became a case in point in the exhibition *Allan Kaprow: Kunst als Leben* (Art as Life) at Haus der Kunst in Munich in 2006. Although Stephanie Rosenthal, who co-curated the show, put it on with the collaboration of Kaprow himself, she explained that it was a thorny idea to do so with an artist who throughout his life 'challenged the validity of attempts to exhibit his works'.[16] In the exhibition, this dilemma was crystallised in a redoing of Kaprow's *18 Happenings in 6 Parts* conceived by writer and curator André Lepecki. While it was possible to replicate quite faithfully the setting of semi-transparent partitions in which the work originally took place in 1959, 'The real problem was that we would be placing *18 Happenings in 6 Parts* inside a museum's gallery – when it was clear that its original location inside an empty loft on Fourth Avenue in Manhattan's East Village was already Kaprow's critique of how art gets to be framed, consumed, accessed', Lepecki pointed out. He summed up, 'the problem was how to de-territorialize our room from the institutional frame of the museum'.[17] At Haus der Kunst, the awkwardness of an institutional redoing of *18 Happenings in 6 Parts* was not only accepted but staged, as it was presented within a big box made of cheap construction materials (which did not lend itself to contemplation, like an artwork would) and was placed at an angle so it did not align with the walls of the gallery. Lepecki explained, 'the redoing could only take place inside a museum's gallery as long as it remained slightly misplaced'.[18]

'Spectacularisation'

In 2013 Sabine Breitwieser noted a shift of the museum 'towards an audience-oriented approach, in which the museum becomes a service provider within a feel-good, event-oriented culture'.[19] With a range of activities taking place in the museum, whether educational programmes for children or dancing parties with DJs, performance was bound to play a part in making it a place where things happen, often on a large scale. 'It is only in the past twenty years that performance art has become "industrialized"', Claire Bishop observed in 2012 as she saw performance moving 'from festival to museum space, mobilizing large numbers of performers, unionized modes of remuneration, and ever larger audiences'.[20]

Against the background of this 'industrialisation', the appeal of performance created suspicion that its sharper edge could be eroded within the clasp of the institution. Lois Keidan assessed in 2014 that, 'the biggest challenge is around the potential depoliticization of an area of practice that is inherently politicized. There is a concern that an institutional embrace will inevitably compromise performance's disruptive intention.'[21] At stake now was the utilisation of performance as part of a strategy to attract crowds in the museum and its manipulation for entertainment purposes, that is to say its 'spectacularisation'. Bishop also highlighted the role played by architecture when she wrote about the Donald B. and Catherine C. Marron Atrium at the Museum of Modern Art in New York. A space of unusual height and pierced to allow a view from several floors, its 'scale and atmosphere of prestige and capital has the unwelcome side effect of making experimental performance look under-rehearsed and unprofessional, rather than intimate and nuanced', she concluded in 2014.[22]

However, performance works, like art of any medium, can be anti-spectacular by nature. Reacting to the performance exhibition *Actions and Interruptions* at Tate Modern in London in 2007, Melanie Gilligan noted, 'Into the museum's cultural-tourism maelstrom were inserted various actions closely resembling the everyday behavior of gallery visitors, with several too lifelike even to garner an audience. Roman Ondak's *Good Feelings in Good Times*, 2003, for instance – a queue leading nowhere – was camouflaged between actual, but similarly interminable, queues for elevators, tickets, and Carsten Holler's slides'[23] (Höller's *Test Site* comprised of huge slides which visitors were invited to use).

It is important to realise that performance has resources of its own to reflect on the conditions of its presentation. Catherine Wood observed in 2018 that in recent developments, 'Performance heightens our perception of art's components: they are making, we are watching, this is the work of art'. She expands, 'in a twenty-first century context, where the optical field is dominated by seductive images on screens, this kind of work puts an emphasis, instead, on the conventional frame of art – the gallery – as not just a viewing space, but a public space in which to gather'.[24] This intensified awareness of the act of looking at art and the context of this experience is illustrated by Stuart Ringholt's 2011 performance *Preceded by a tour of the show by artist Stuart Ringholt, 6–8pm. The artist will be naked. Those who wish to join the tour must also be naked. Adults only.* First presented at the Museum of Contemporary Art Australia in Sydney after it entered its collection, the piece is a gallery tour led, outside of the museum's opening hours, by the artist, with the specification that both he and the spectators have to be in the nude, provoking a shift of awareness from the subject of the tour (works on display) to one's own and others' nakedness, to the experience of strangers looking at art together, while also, possibly, changing the perception of the works.

Dancing Exhibitions

Evoking the place given to performance in the museum
in the 1980s and 1990s, Pablo Bronstein has written,
'Once every couple of years, as a peripheral event related
to a solo exhibition, an artist, dressed in a suit, might bang
a hammer against a piece of wood for two hours in front
of a delighted audience'.[25] While his description is humorously
exaggerated, his account of performance being programmed
as a 'peripheral event' did reflect the situation back then, and
also in the following years. Catherine Wood has explained
that in the festival of performance *Live Culture* at Tate Modern
in London in 2003, she found 'problematic ... the way it was
ring-fenced as a separate "event", not part of the so-called
"core programme"'. She noted, 'Although it was *in* the
institution, it wasn't *really* getting in there'.[26]

Reacting to this compartmentalisation, one of the concerns
of curators was to desegregate performance within the museum.
Departing from the principle of live performance being added
to museums' programmes as one-off events, a significant
evolution was the assimilation of live works into the model
of the exhibition. This adhesion of performance to the visual-
art format that is the exhibition became particularly explicit
when dance was brought into the equation. Reflecting in 2014
on how dance started to appear 'so predominantly in museums',
Mark Franko and André Lepecki asked, 'what does dance have
to gain, or what positive changes may come to dance, once
it starts to move in museums?'[27] The question, of course,
could be reversed, to interrogate the benefits to the museum
of engaging in a close relationship with dance.

The oxymoronic character of *Une Exposition chorégraphiée*
(A Choreographed Exhibition) was flaunted in this exhibition
of 'movements' curated by Mathieu Copeland at the Kunsthalle
in St Gallen in 2007–8. Live works by artists (among them
Roman Ondak) and choreographers (Jonah Bokaer, for example)

were shown in an otherwise empty gallery throughout the opening hours of the Kunsthalle. It was an early example of what Claire Bishop has called 'performance exhibitions', a genre characterised by 'the adaptation and prolongation of performance to fill museum spaces and opening hours'.[28] This type of curatorial exercise gained prominence in this period, perhaps giving performers the feeling of being fully at home in the museum, rather than making a stealth appearance. The adaptation of the presentation of live works to the time and space constraints of the exhibition was the work of curators and artists, as well as, to a significant extent, choreographers, who were, Bishop has explained, 'willing to adjust their stage works to gallery spaces in order to reach bigger, more diverse audiences'.[29]

In the 2010s dance enjoyed increasing exposure in the museum, in the process, crucially, stretching the definition of the exhibition. By adopting the model of the exhibition, it departed from the compartmentalisation of space induced by the stage and from the organisation of time which is that of the theatre. At the Fundació Antoni Tàpies in Barcelona in 2012, the choreographer Xavier Le Roy had a 'retrospective', tentatively named as such between inverted commas in the title of the exhibition *'Retrospectiva' de Xavier Le Roy*. For two months, dancers performed throughout the day, in the empty main gallery, extracts of solo pieces by Le Roy, while in another room video archives were available for consultation.

The trend of museums looking at new modes of presentation of live works through dance was also noticeable when the Museum of Modern Art in New York invited the choreographer Boris Charmatz to show dance pieces over three consecutive weekends in 2013. The title of the event, *Musée de la danse: Three Collective Gestures*, referred to the Musée de la danse (Museum of Dance) in Rennes, France, of which Charmatz was the Director, and suggested the idea of the art museum hosting not just an event but also another institution. Two years later, another 'dancing exhibition' organised by Charmatz, scheduled at Tate Modern in London over two days, suggested even more explicitly a conflation of identities, even a transitioning, under the title *If Tate Modern was Musée de la danse?*

The Musée de la danse was itself a composite entity that sat between the models of the museum and the theatre, Charmatz having renamed the choreographic centre as a 'museum' when taking up the reins in 2009. He saw this institution as 'a place where one can go, like in the case of a museum, without knowing in advance the day's programme',[30] and encounter liveness in the form of rehearsals, workshops or discussions, rather than as a one-off event. The Musée de la danse was meant to be experienced, like a museum, through a visit (rather than a show to attend) that would not be at a set time or fixed by a numbered seat (or by any seat at all). Dance institutions proved as eager to make themselves open to the museum's modes of operation as the museum was keen to be associated with the liveness of dance centres. In 2018 the French national dance institution Centre national de la danse in Pantin, near Paris, invited museums to literally transform the dance centre into a 'living museum' for three weekends. Fundação de Serralves, Art Institute of Chicago, Magasin des Horizons in Grenoble, Musée éphémère de la mode in Paris and Centro de Arte Reina Sofía in Madrid all took part in this initiative, titled *L'invitation aux musées* (Invitation to Museums).

Live Exhibitions

In an echo of the presence of dance in the museum, performance started to be shown to a significant extent in continuous displays akin to those featuring objects, and often amongst them. Framing a series of performance works as an exhibition involved the visibility of these works on par, as much as possible, with those hanging on the walls, sitting on plinths or placed on the floor. This visibility could be achieved through a frequency of events sustained during the entire duration of the exhibition. In *Local Positioning Systems* in 2012, for example, live works were presented in various spaces of the Museum of Contemporary Art Australia in Sydney over two months, a period equating to the time span of an exhibition. This aligned the performance series to the standard display model of the museum.

At the Museo de Arte Latinoamericano de Buenos Aires, *Experiencia Infinita* (Infinite Experience) was conceived in 2015 to ponder the question, 'Is a live museum – where the works act, speak, move about, and live eternally – possible?'[31] Performances were shown in different rooms, which allowed a simultaneity of events and evoked the usual distribution of works in the different parts of an exhibition. Occasional interactions occurred as a result. For example, a performer wearing a mask made of very bright lightbulbs navigated the galleries (Pierre Huyghe, *Player*, 2010). When this performer passed through the room where another performer sitting at a desk was describing on a computer what they saw around them and the text was projected on a large screen (Dora García, *Narrativa instantánea*, 2006), the masked wanderer became part of the 'instant narrative' of the exhibition.

No preferred or standard format has emerged in the variety of plans laid out for 'live exhibitions'. Arrangements made to accommodate live works vary tremendously in their utilisation of architecture and timing, resulting in great differences in duration, pace, deployment of space and intensity, and in the choice whether to isolate performance in its own room or to show it amongst other works. The number of these exhibitions and their variety testify to a hunger for experimentation. In 2018 the exhibition *New Swiss Performance Now* exclusively comprised performances, more than fifty of them crammed into a very tight schedule. On the first floor of the Kunsthalle Basel, they were presented consecutively, and sometimes simultaneously, every opening day within a one-month programme that did not allow any breaks. For the exhibition of work by the choreographer Adam Linder, entitled *Hustle Harder* (Museum of Contemporary Art Australia, Sydney, 2023) and also one month long, the presentation of live pieces amongst works on display in the galleries throughout opening hours was made possible by the hiring of nine dancers who performed in rotation. As for Dora García's retrospective *She Has Many Names*, held at the Museum van Hedendaagse Kunst (Museum of Contemporary Art) in Antwerp in 2023, which also included installations and films, a calendar of live performances presented at specific times operated throughout the exhibition.

In these shows that put performance in the foreground, the museum itself appeared as a focal point. These exhibitions were manifestations of introspective endeavours by which the museum tested its capacity to change, morph and adapt. Such reflection on its identity was epitomised by the proposition made by Fundação de Serralves in Porto to think about 'The Museum as Performance'. Since its creation in 2015, this annual event has offered, over the course of a weekend, a programme of performances taking place in the galleries, the atrium, the auditorium or the surrounding park. In the 2023 edition, André Guedes made the audience very aware of the setting in which his work *Canção nova* (New Song, 2023) took place, namely the auditorium, as access to the room was modified and the audience had their chairs pulled away by the performers. In addition, a choir singing folk songs and images of rehearsals referred to another institution, the theatre Teatro Aberto in Lisbon.

THE PRAGMATIC MUSEUM

Filling Gaps in Research

Exhibitions have long been a driving force for research, and accompanying catalogues an opportunity to advance scholarship. Museums started to become aware of significant lacunae in the knowledge of performance when large exhibitions were mounted in the 1990s, and it was not a case of empty words when Kathy Halbreich wrote in 1993 that the catalogue of *In the Spirit of Fluxus* was conceived as 'an attempt to fill a gap in scholarship'.[32] For the most comprehensive exhibitions, addressing overlooked parts of the history of performance

has required an enormous amount of research, a situation
Jay Sanders was confronted with when he was working
on the exhibition *Rituals of Rented Island: Object Theater,
Loft Performance, and the New Psychodrama – Manhattan,
1970–1980* at the Whitney Museum of American Art, New York,
in 2013–14. He explained, 'My colleague Greta Hartenstein
and I had to do a great deal of primary research because
many of those artists did not have a clear written history'.[33]

In the 2010s there was a significant research dimension
associated with exhibitions laying the groundwork for the
history of performance in particular periods or regions,
or honing this history. At the Centro de Arte Reina Sofía
in Madrid in 2013, Fluxus was examined through the lens
of a single year in the exhibition *± 1961: Founding the Expanded
Arts*, while at Garage Museum of Contemporary Art in Moscow
in 2014, most of the 20th century was encompassed in *Russian
Performance: A Cartography of its History*, a large exhibition
that covered the period from Russian Futurism to the work
of contemporary artists such as Petr Pavlensky. In addition
to the publication of a catalogue, archival material was made
available online. *Russian Performance* was the culmination
of a burst of activity around performance at Garage, which
had been kickstarted by the organisation of the exhibition
33 Fragments of Russian Performance for the Performa Hub
in New York in 2011. This momentum at Garage also translated
into the conference *Performance Art: Ethics in Action* in 2013.

In parallel, and sometimes in conjunction, with exhibitions
were launched research programmes specifically geared
towards performance. These initiatives, increasingly coming
into existence as online resources, often revolved around
the examination of the engagement of the museum with
performance. The project Polish Performance Archive was
developed around performance-related works acquired
by the Muzeum Sztuki Nowoczesnej in Warsaw, which also
organised the symposium *Performance as the Paradigm of Art*
in 2013. Studying performance was the focus of the texts
published online by the Walker Art Center in Minneapolis

in 2014 (*Living Collections Catalogue*) and by Tate in 2016 (*Performance at Tate: Into the Space of Art*), both projects looking at specific cases and situations encountered by these institutions. In the former, for example, Elizabeth Carpenter pondered how the Walker Art Center 'might go about transforming its acquisition strategies to include the collection of not only "performative objects" but performance itself'.[34] In these publications, the question of the particular problems posed by live works resurfaced again and again. Carpenter acknowledged in the introduction to the first volume of *Living Collections Catalogue* that it had 'generated more questions than answers.'[35]

Performance Anxiety

'*How Are We Performing Today?*' the Museum of Modern Art in New York asked itself in 2012 in a symposium subtitled *New Formats, Places, and Practices of Performance-Related Art*. The double meaning of the word 'performing' indicated an emulation, and perhaps a need for reassurance. As live performance was becoming a fixture of contemporary art museum events and exhibitions, and the process of collecting live works was well underway, the question of the sustainability of these works over time was being raised with pressing need. It became intrinsically clear that the acquisition, conservation and presentation of live performance were entangled.

In the 2010s discussions on performance in the museum shifted from debates largely sparked by the wave of re-enactments and dominated by scholars to a no less rigorous and ambitious but significantly more pragmatic affair. Working on the front line and motivated by their experience of the problems posed by live works were museum staff such as curators and conservators. They took the lead in debates as symposiums and workshops were organised with a certain sense of urgency. While the discussions initiated by the museum were informed by the long-term vision of its mission vis-à-vis performance, their first aim was to figure out practical

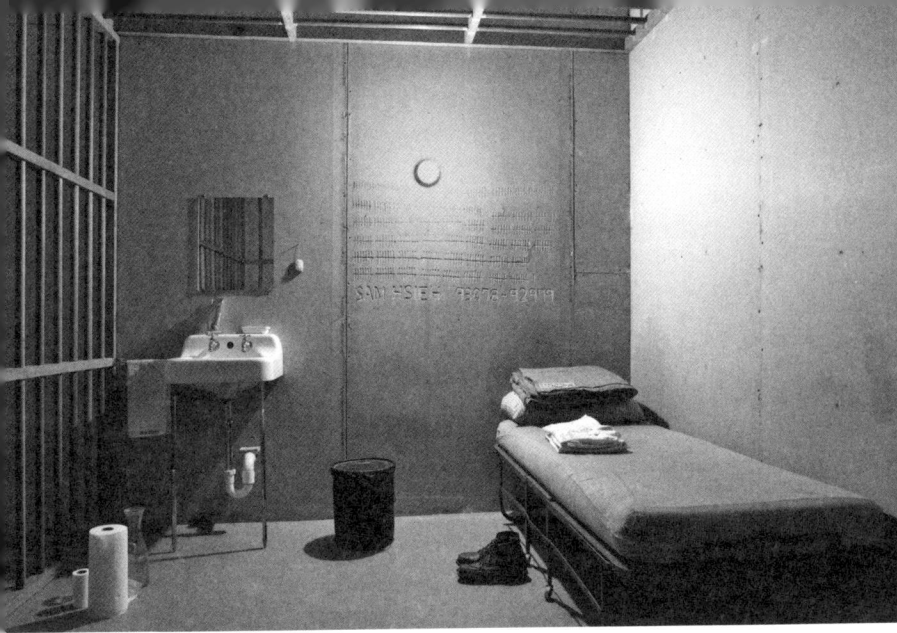

Fig.20 Tehching Hsieh, *Cage Piece*, 1978–9, installation view of the exhibition *Performance 1: Tehching Hsieh*, The Museum of Modern Art, New York, 21 January–18 May 2009

solutions for immediate implementation. The appetite for dialogue and consultation on performance seemed designed for prompt and actual methods and solutions to be applied to exhibition, conservation and acquisition procedures.

As early as 2008, the Museum of Modern Art in New York gathered artists, conservators, curators and scholars for a series of private workshops whose aim was to reflect on the way performance could be conserved and collected. These workshops appear to have prepared the ground for the acquisition of live works (three entered the museum's collection in 2009, marking an acceleration of this type of activity). They also preceded initiatives such as the 'Performance Exhibition Series', inaugurated in 2009 with a show on Tehching Hsieh featuring photographs and posters, and whose set piece was the original cell the artist built in his studio and within which he spent a year with little more than a bed and a sink (*Cage Piece*, 1978–9, fig.20). The 'Performance Exhibition Series' was initially meant to culminate with Marina Abramović's retrospective *The Artist is Present* in 2010, but the series was extended to the following year. In 2010 the Guggenheim Museum in New York held a symposium titled *Thinking Performance at the Guggenheim*, framing the reflection on the institution itself. The same year, it mounted the exhibition *Haunted: Contemporary Photography / Video / Performance*, as well as organising a Tino Sehgal exhibition and acquiring one of his works.

This evolution occurred as it was becoming increasingly common for performance works to be made specifically for the museum, using the institution as a stakeholder which could provide logistical, financial and human resources. The conservator Pip Laurenson recalled in 2023 that when she worked with the exhibition team at what was then the Tate Gallery in London, in the early 1990s, 'the degree to which artists would tenaciously hold to their vision to overcome complex logistical or technical problems was striking to me. It is something that is rarely examined in the discourse of contemporary art, except in occasionally sensational terms'.[36] The fact that performance works, presented as part of exhibitions or acquired for collections, could be created or presented in close collaboration with the museum, prompted the need for recommendations to be made, guidelines to be set up and procedures to be established. The motivation for the examination of the museum's state vis-à-vis performance was above all practical.

A brainchild of Tate and Van Abbemuseum that came to fruition in 2014, 'The Live List: What to Consider when Collecting Live Works' was the first project of its kind and offered a range of questions to be considered in the process of the acquisition, presentation and conservation of live works. While discussions held for two years on the topic of 'Collecting the Performative' in preparation for this project focused on theoretical issues such as 'authorship, authenticity, autonomy, documentation, memory, continuity and liveness',[37] the document which emerged from this process as The Live

List addressed very practical questions such as the auditioning of performers, the duration of the work, rehearsals, the status of props, lighting, acoustics, documentation, cost and museum staff. 'Are the props consumed or destroyed during the performance?', and 'What does the HR department need to take care of? Shifts? Pay? Rules for dealing with illness, absence?' were among the questions the document asked.[38]

At the Walker Art Center in Minneapolis in 2011, a discussion on the question of collecting performance navigated how to keep record of the steps of a live work (including before and after its presentation), given the fact that performance is 'by nature slippery – the work exists only in the moment of its enactment' and is 'inherently fickle', museum professional Susannah Schouweiler reported.[39] Curators and other professionals were invited to ponder this question at an event timed to reflect on the recent acquisition of a large number of objects from the Merce Cunningham Dance Company. A common thread for the participants in the debate, Schouweiler wrote, was the idea that 'capturing' the history of a live work 'involves not only collecting the sets, props, costumes, and media recordings of the event, but also artists' notes, scores, and documentation of script readings, workshops, and open rehearsals'.[40]

If amassing information on a performance during acquisition is essential to define its consistency, it is also an opportunity to identify its variability over past iterations. This process is likely to be repeated at each new presentation. Space, time, material components, logistics and, increasingly, the role and place of the audience are among the parameters on which information is added and consigned over time. While Louise Lawson, Acatia Finbow and Hélia Marçal examined these different stages in the research project 'Strategy for the Documentation and Conservation of Performance' (2018) at Tate, they insisted on the key role played by each presentation. They wrote, 'The nature of performance-based artworks, their oscillation between being active and dormant in a way that no other type of artwork fully endures, means that it is only when they are performed that we can understand their conservation needs'.[41] One implication of this is that the lack of presentation of a performance after its acquisition compromises its conservation. As a live work enters a collection it triggers a domino effect, engaging the museum in a cycle binding together acquisition, conservation and presentation.

The Transmission of the Intangible

Procedures of acquisition and conservation specifically devised by museum professionals to steward performance over time emerged against a tradition of expertise developed around objects, rather than intangible heritage. 'Western institutions of art and culture have long discredited or actively suppressed the practices of oral history, body-to-body transmission and ritual inheritance that are so crucial to performance's longevity', write Hanna B. Hölling, Jules Pelta Feldman and Emilie Magnin.[42] It is precisely this type of immaterial transmission that is put into practice by Tino Sehgal as he requires that the formalisation of the acquisition of his 'constructed situations' be done verbally, in line with the principle that his work does not generate the production of anything material. In the light of this, the transfer of ownership involves a number of people including Sehgal or a member of his studio, curators, conservators, registrars, and possibly a lawyer, all engaged in stating the terms of the transaction, witnessing it, guaranteeing its legality and memorising the instructions. An important effect of the reliance on memorisation, rather than written stipulations, is that the conservation of the work cannot be based on a template that would be permanently enshrined. As Dorothea von Hantelmann says, 'There is indeed a clearly defined way to execute the work, but, because there is no fixed original, the respective individual way of interpreting it co-defines the work'.[43]

Sehgal's approach draws attention to the nature of transmission and the role played by people other than the artist in this process. It points, in particular, to the importance of individual memory, of eminently subjective mental impressions. In bypassing documentation entirely in the acquisition, presentation and conservation of his works, Sehgal's approach transfers new obligations to the museum. The artist passes the memory of the work on to the museum, which in turn is responsible for passing it on to performers, who themselves build a mental and physical impression of the piece. The immaterial procedure put in place by Sehgal heightens individual responsibility, not the least that of playing one's part in keeping alive the memory of a work. Only two years after Sehgal's *Kiss* was acquired by the Museum of Modern Art in New York in 2008, Sydney Briggs, a registrar at the museum, confided to Vivian van Saaze, 'now that Tino is off doing new pieces, new works, how do we help the interpreters to maintain this memory? Because if a dancer works less, if you cannot actually dance and repeat a choreography, you will forget it. As we cannot record it, they cannot look at it and really have to remember it.'[44] Long-term inertia, the case of Sehgal suggests, is not only detrimental to the conservation of the work but can put its very existence at risk.

While the conditions of the transmission of Sehgal's works are specific to him, his philosophy sheds light on the role of staff and the compartmentalisation of responsibilities and expertise in the museum. Once a live work has been integrated into a collection, should its conservation only be the job of conservators? The Museum of Modern Art in New York acquired in 2015 Simone Forti's *Dance Constructions* (1960–1), a series of dance works using objects and involving ordinary movements such as standing, walking or climbing. Athena Christa Holbrook has explained how, following this acquisition, she travelled in 2016 to Vleeshal, in the Netherlands, as Collection Specialist of the Department of Media and Performance Art, to document rehearsals for the exhibition *Here It Comes*. To her surprise, she was invited to take part in the rehearsals, becoming the 'institutional memory' of the work. She wrote, 'In stepping into the role of performer, these performances have become part of my physical memory –

I am both archivist and archive, documentarian and documented, a vessel for receiving movement and for transmitting it'.[45] As institutional and personal memories blend, transmission becomes a question of knowledge that is theoretical as much as experiential and embodied, a responsibility that is collective as much as personal. As Boris Charmatz has explained about collecting live dance, 'The body is the most active storage room, educated by gestures, full of memory, ready to be activated for the present and future'.[46]

The complexity of the conservation of live works exposes potential limits to their acquisition. A visual art institution does not necessarily have the in-house expertise, space or financial means to organise regular workshops and presentations. In response to such challenges, the Museum of Modern Art in New York collaborated with the dance centre Danspace Project in 2016 to ensure the transfer of the memory of Simone Forti's *Dance Constructions*. During a week-long residency in New York, Forti herself as well as dancers and other guests worked together. One of the performers, Talya Epstein, explained how Forti 'gives us all the space and time so that our group dynamic can unfold without too much outside meddling. Every now and then she will add a directive, like "place a hand on someone as they pass" but this feels more like a suggestion and dissent is welcome.'[47] As Holbrook has written, 'Perhaps delegated communal performance necessitates delegated communal conservation',[48] suggesting a transfer, or partial transfer, of conservation to other institutions.

Conclusion

In the variety of exchanges between performance and the museum since the 1960s one finds outbursts of anger, acts of defiance, repression and rebellion, as well as a great deal of discussion, collaboration and mutual assistance. Artists and museum professionals have worked together and looked at, for example, how to establish the parameters of a live work for its acquisition, combine objects and documents and organise their display, or figure out the practicalities of the reconstruction of performance sets. This relationship has had profound effects on the museum as it has appointed specialists, embarked on years-long research programmes, made room for performers among paintings and sculptures or prudently emptied galleries altogether, fished for ideas and propositions in dance centres and choreographers, and thoroughly redefined conservation and acquisition procedures, if not the notions of conservation and acquisition themselves.

Behind the mobilisation and the buzz, difficulties have nonetheless persisted as well as complications that are specific to the immaterial nature of performance. Perhaps the most emblematic of these problems is psychological and lies, in terms of acquisition, in the act of buying nothing but the possibility of an action. This operation amounts to a leap of faith that can still easily appear unreasonably speculative and hazardous. This is all the more the case with public institutions that are accountable for their spending. Some museum stakeholders may simply balk at paying for something intangible, Guggenheim Museum curator Nat Trotman claimed in 2019. 'Donors, patrons, trustees, people who are outside of the curators but who are vetting and approving acquisitions still aren't entirely comfortable with the idea of collecting something that ostensibly is not a *thing*.'[1]

Beyond this psychological resistance, one of the main obstacles to the presence of live works in the museum today may be a simple question of money. A performance without props does not need to be wrapped, encased and transported, but its production can be expensive. The hiring of performers usually makes up the lion's share of the overall cost, and the price increases for presentations stretching over a long period of time – the traditional two-month period of a museum exhibition, for example. In addition, questions as diverse as the number of people that should be hired, if rotations are necessary, the skills they need to have or the clothes they should wear must be addressed by a great variety of staff, and possibly in conversation with the artist. As Claire Bishop observed in 2012, 'If body art in the '60s and '70s was produced quickly and inexpensively (since the artist's own body was the cheapest form of material), delegated performance today, by contrast, tends to be a luxury game'.[2]

Although performance can be acquired relatively cheaply in relation to other works of art that come onto the market, the range of costs which are induced and of human resources which are mobilised can drastically limit the number of live pieces owned and presented by an institution. Two performers were necessary for *Fault Lines* (2013), a work by Jennifer Allora and Guillermo Calzadilla which was acquired by the Museum of Modern Art in New York in 2016, but its presentation required auditions to find two young boys able to perform a duet and selected for their voice range, vocal coaches to be hired, rehearsals to be held, and the boys making themselves available during the museum's opening hours. Planning this could take a whole year. 'Even many of the groundbreaking institutions that helped write this history through their innovative exhibitions and collections policies now struggle to keep up', curator Sabine Breitwieser wrote in 2019.[3] The risk, of course, is that the number of museums able to afford such 'luxury games' is reduced to a bare minimum. If this actually happens, Breitwieser asserts, 'we will have to conclude that media-specific hierarchies that once dominated art have been merely transferred externally to create a hierarchical relationship among institutions instead'.[4]

More optimistically, the presence of performance in collections has also proved an opportunity to ponder the very idea of ownership in museums that are predominantly organised around categories – of works and staff – devised for fixed objects. 'Can an institution divorce the notion of "ownership" from exclusivity?' curator Philip Bither asked in 2016, going on to say that, 'Perhaps it is time to *attempt to transform the lexicon of the museum*, further challenging the disciplinary lines that continue to feel rigid, as well as examining the distinctions of value that populate the visual and performing art worlds in such different ways'.[5] What Bither had in mind was an approach to collecting developed by the Walker Art Center in Minneapolis, whereby it acquires a single presentation of a live work, rather than the work itself. This conception of ownership is based on stewardship rather than exclusive rights, a way of emphasising the role of commissions in the programme of the art centre. *Scaffold Room* (2014), for example, is a performance that the Walker Art Center commissioned from Ralph Lemon, acquiring in 2015 only the specific iteration of the work that was presented there. As Breitwieser observes, the key question is 'whether the concept of the museum – and the notions of ownership and rights that are inherent within this structure – can actually be uncoupled from its original hegemonic conditions. And if it is possible, we must ask whether or not the museum runs the risk of losing its authority and its identity.'[6]

Notes

FOREWORD

1   'Martin Creed Work No. 850, Duveens Commission', Tate website,
    https://www.tate.org.uk/whats-on/tate-britain/martin-creed-work
    -no-850, accessed 9 January 2025.
2   In Charlotte Higgins, 'Tate Exhibit Keeps on Running', *The Guardian*,
    30 June 2008, https://www.theguardian.com/artanddesign/2008
    /jun/30/art.tatebritain, accessed 9 January 2025.

INTRODUCTION

1   Marta Minujín, 'Destruction of My Works in the Impasse Ronsin, Paris'
    (1963), translated by Marguerite Feitlowitz, in *Listen Here Now! Argentine Art
    of the 1960s: Writings of the Avant-Garde*, edited by Inés Katzenstein, Museum
    of Modern Art, New York, and Thames & Hudson, London, 2004, p.59.
2   Dore Ashton in the press release of *Homage to New York*, Museum of
    Modern Art, New York, 1960, https://www.moma.org/momaorg/shared
    /pdfs/docs/press_archives/2634/releases/MOMA_1960_0033_27.pdf,
    accessed 8 February 2024.
3   Amelia Jones, *Body Art / Performing the Subject*, University of Minnesota
    Press, Minneapolis, 1998, p.13.

CHAPTER 1

1   RoseLee Goldberg, 'Performance: Art for All?', *Art Journal*, vol.40,
    nos 1–2, Autumn–Winter 1980, p.369.
2   Lawrence Alloway, 'Introduction', *Eleven from the Reuben Gallery*,
    New York, 1965, n.p.
3   Gustav Metzger, quoted in Kristine Stiles, *The Destruction in Art Symposium
    (DIAS): The Radical Cultural Project of Event-Structured Live Art*, University
    of California, Berkeley, 1987, p.250.
4   Jenevive Nykolak, 'On Moving and Touching: From Kineticism to
    Dance in the Museum', *Art Journal*, vol.78, no.4, Winter 2019, p.44.
5   Billy Klüver, in B. Klüver and Robert Rauschenberg, 'Art in Motion
    – A Combined Memory', *Konsthistorisk tidskrift / Journal of Art History*,
    vol.76, nos 1–2, 2007, p.117.
6   Oscar Masotta, 'I Committed a Happening', in Katzenstein (ed.),
    op.cit., p.197.
7   Allan Kaprow (1967), quoted in *Allan Kaprow: Art as Life*, edited

by Eva Meyer-Hermann, Andrew Perchuk and Stephanie Rosenthal, Getty Research Institute, Los Angeles, 2008, p.76.

8   Patricia Falguières, 'Institution, Invention, Possibility', in *How Institutions Think: Between Contemporary Art and Curatorial Discourse*, edited by Paul O'Neill, Lucy Steeds and Mick Wilson, The MIT Press, Cambridge, MA, 2017, p.31.

9   Brian O'Doherty, *Inside the White Cube: The Ideology of the Gallery Space*, Lapis Press, Santa Monica, 1986, p.107.

10 Hélio Oiticica, 'Position and Program' (1966), in *Hélio Oiticica*, Witte de With Center for Contemporary Art, Rotterdam, and Galerie nationale du Jeu de Paume, Paris, 1992, pp 103-4.

11 Pablo Suárez, 'Letter of Resignation' (1968), translated by Albert G. Bork, in Katzenstein (ed.), op.cit., p.290.

12 Oscar Bony (1998), quoted in and translated by Andrea Giunta, 'An Aesthetic of Discontinuity', in *Oscar Bony, El mago: Obras 1965-2001*, Fundación Eduardo F. Costantini, Buenos Aires, 2007, p.272.

13 Oscar Bony, quoted in Victoria Giraudo, 'Cronología Biográfica', in *Oscar Bony: El Mago*, op.cit., p.213.

14 Lucy R. Lippard, 'Biting the Hand: Artists and Museums in New York since 1969', in *Alternative Art, New York, 1965-1985: A Cultural Politics Book for the Social Text Collective*, edited by Julie Ault, University of Minnesota Press, Minneapolis, 2002, p.80.

15 ibid., p.79.

16 *Stuart Brisley*, Institute of Contemporary Arts, London, 1981, p.19.

17 Claudia Calirman, *Brazilian Art under Dictatorship: Antonio Manuel, Artur Barrio, and Cildo Meireles*, Duke University Press, Durham, NC, 2012, p.38.

18 Jay Sanders, 'Whitney Museum of American Art, New York. Jay Sanders, Engell Speyer Family Curator and Curator of Performance: In Conversation with Jonah Westerman, April 2015', *Histories of Performance Documentation: Museum, Artistic, and Scholarly Practices*, edited by Gabriella Giannachi and Jonah Westerman, Routledge, London and New York, 2018, p.21.

19 Allan Kaprow, *Assemblage, Environments & Happenings*, Harry N. Abrams, New York, 1966, p.150.

20 Jürgen Becker and Wolf Vostell, *Happenings, Fluxus, Pop Art, Nouveau Réalisme: Eine Dokumentation*, Rowohlt, Hamburg, 1965; Claes Oldenburg and Emmet Williams, *Store Days: Documents from The Store (1961) and Ray Gun Theater (1962)*, Something Else Press, New York, 1967.

21 Eva Meyer-Hermann, 'Museum as Mediation', in *Allan Kaprow: Art as Life*, op.cit., p.77.

22 Harald Szeemann, 'How Does an Exhibition Come into Being?' (19 November 1968), in *Exhibiting the New Art: 'Op Losse Schroeven' and 'When Attitudes Become Form' 1969*, edited by Christian Rattemeyer, Afterall Books, London, in association with The Academy of Fine Arts Vienna and Van Abbemuseum, Eindhoven, 2010, p.176.

23 Jean-Marc Poinsot, 'Large Exhibitions: A Sketch of a Typology' (1986), translated by Robert McGee, in *Thinking About Exhibitions*, edited by Reesa Greenberg, Bruce W. Ferguson and Sandy Nairne, Routledge, London, 1996, pp 49-50.

24 Harald Szeemann, letter to George Brecht, 21 January 1970, Harald
    Szeemann Papers, Box 296, Folder 3, Getty Research Institute, Los Angeles.
25 Harald Szeeman (1988), quoted in Hans-Joachim Müller, *Harald Szeemann:*
    Exhibition Maker, Hatje Cantz, Ostfildern-Ruit, 2006, p.30.
26 Harald Szeemann interviewed by Jean-Pierre Bordaz, in *Hors limites:*
    L'art et la vie, 1952–1994, Centre Georges Pompidou, Paris, 1994,
    p.265 (author's translation).
27 Letter from Harald Szeemann to John Gibson, 15 November 1970,
    Harald Szeemann Papers, Box 296, Folder 11, Getty Research Institute,
    Los Angeles.
28 Lucy Lippard, *Six Years: The Dematerialization of the Art Object from 1966*
    to 1972 (1973), University of California Press, Berkeley, 1997, p.17.
29 Vito Acconci, 'Some Notes on Activity and Performance' (1969),
    in *Vito Acconci*, edited by Mark C. Taylor, Frazer Ward and Jennifer
    Bloomer, Phaidon, London, 2002, p.92.
30 Vito Acconci, 'Service Area', in *Information*, edited by Kynaston
    L. McShine, Museum of Modern Art, New York, 1970, p.5.
31 Michel Foucault, *Discipline and Punish: The Birth of the Prison* (1975),
    translated by Alan Sheridan, Penguin, London, 1991, p.154.
32 Andrée Hayum, 'Note on Performance and the Arts', *Art Journal*,
    vol.XXXIV, no.4, Summer 1975, p.338.

CHAPTER 2

1   RoseLee Goldberg, 'Performance: The Golden Years', in *The Art*
    of Performance: A Critical Anthology, edited by Gregory Battcock and
    Robert Nickas, Dutton, New York, 1984, pp 71–94.
2   Jean-Marc Poinsot, 'Large Exhibitions: A Sketch of a Typology',
    in *Thinking about Exhibitions*, op.cit., p.41.
3   François Barré, 'Avant-propos', in *Hors limites*, op.cit., p.11
    (author's translation).
4   Paul Schimmel (1998), quoted in Frazer Ward, 'The Real Thing', *Frieze*,
    no.41, June–August 1998, p.47.
5   Allan Kaprow (1996), quoted in Stephanie Rosenthal, 'Agency for Action',
    in *Allan Kaprow: Art as Life*, op.cit., p.62.
6   Milena Tomic, 'Reinvention as Parallax: Allegorical and Other Afterlives
    of Allan Kaprow's Un-Art', *Word & Image*, vol.33, no.2, April–June 2017,
    p.118.
7   Michael Rush, 'A Noisy Silence', *PAJ: A Journal of Performance and Art*,
    vol.21, no.1, January 1999, p.2.
8   Ward, 'The Real Thing', op.cit., p.47.
9   For example, *Fluxus: Selections from the Gilbert and Lila Silverman Collection*,
    The Museum of Modern Art Library, New York, 1988–9; *Ubi Fluxus Ibi*
    Motus 1990–1962, Ex Granai della Repubblica alle Zitelle, Venice, 1990; and
    FluxAttitudes, The New Museum of Contemporary Art, New York, 1992–3.
10 Kristine Stiles, 'Between Water and Stone. Fluxus Performance:
    A Metaphysics of Acts', in *In the Spirit of Fluxus*, Walker Art Center,
    Minneapolis, 1993, p.65.

11   Anonymous, untitled, *The Print Collector's Newsletter*, vol.11, no.3, July–August 1980, p.105.

12   Vito Acconci, in Jan Avgikos, 'Interview: Vito Acconci', *Art Papers*, vol.5, no.1, January–February 1981, n.p.

13   B[arbara] H[askell], 'Acknowledgments', in *Blam!: The Explosion of Pop, Minimalism, and Performance 1958–1964*, Whitney Museum of American Art, New York, in association with W.W. Norton & Company, 1984, p.9.

14   Arthur Danto, 'Blam!: The Explosion of Pop, Minimalism, and Performance 1958–1964', *The Nation*, 20 October 1984, p.391.

15   Jennifer Mundy, 'Why / Why Not Replicate?', *Tate Papers*, no.8, Autumn 2007, https://www.tate.org.uk/research/publications/tate-papers/08/whywhy-not-replicate, accessed 19 May 2020.

16   Alex Potts, 'The Enduringly Ephemeral', *Tate Papers*, no.8, Autumn 2007, https://www.tate.org.uk/research/publications/tate-papers/08/the-enduringly-ephemeral, accessed 26 March 2020.

17   Salvador Muñoz-Viñas, *Contemporary Theory of Conservation*, Routledge, London, 2015, p.1.

18   Robin Kathleen Williams, 'A Mode of Translation: Joan Jonas's Performance Installations', *Stedelijk Studies*, no.3, Fall 2015, 'The Place of Performance', https://stedelijkstudies.com/journal/a-mode-of-translation-joan-jonass-performance-installations/, accessed 19 May 2020.

19   See 'Meredith Monk Reflects on 16 Millimeter Earrings', interview with Senior Curator Siri Engberg, Walker Art Center, 3 October 2018, https://walkerart.org/magazine/meredith-monk-reflects-on-16-millimeter-earrings, accessed 10 October 2023.

20   Marina Abramović, in Nancy Spector, 'Marina Abramović Interviewed', May 2006, in *Seven Easy Pieces*, Edizioni Charta, Milan and New York, 2007, p.16.

21   Rosalind Krauss, 'The Cultural Logic of the Late Capitalist Museum', *October*, vol.54, Autumn 1990, p.6.

22   Sven Lütticken, 'From Re- to Pre- and Back Again', in *Over and Over and Over Again: Reenactment Strategies in Contemporary Arts and Theory*, edited by Cristina Baldacci, Clio Nicastro and Arianna Sforzini, ICI Berlin Press, Berlin, 2022, p.8.

23   Muñoz-Viñas, *Contemporary Theory of Conservation*, op.cit., p.147.

24   See Nathalie Zonnenberg, *Conceptual Art in a Curatorial Perspective: Between Dematerialization and Documentation*, Valiz, Amsterdam, 2019, p.135.

25   Muñoz-Viñas, *Contemporary Theory of Conservation*, op.cit., p.147.

26   Alex Farquharson, 'Action Replay: Live Museum Events', *Frieze*, no.77, September 2003, p.52.

27   ibid.

28   Jens Hoffmann, 'A Certain Tendency of Curating', in *Curating Subjects*, edited by Paul O'Neil, Open Editions, London, 2007, p.141.

29   Claire Bishop, 'Antagonism and Relational Aesthetics', *October*, vol.110, Fall 2004, p.51.

30   ibid., p.52.

31   Anonymous, 'Introduction', in *A Short History of Performance – Part One*, Whitechapel Art Gallery, London, 2002, n.p.

32   Anna Dezeuze, 'Meat Joy', *Art Monthly*, no.257, June 2002, p.2.

33   Carolee Schneemann, quoted in ibid., p.1.

34 Sarah Whitfield, 'London: Performance Art', *The Burlington Magazine*, vol.44, no.1191, June 2002, p.366.

35 Rachel Withers, 'A Short History of Performance: Part One: Whitechapel Gallery', *Artforum*, vol.41, no.1, September 2002, p.215.

36 Jens Hoffmann, quoted in Jennifer Allen, 'Performance Anxiety', *Artforum*, vol.40, no.7, March 2002, p.42.

37 Tino Sehgal, quoted in ibid.

38 Jennifer Allen, '"Einmal ist keinmal": Observations on Reenactment', in *Life, Once More: Forms of Reenactment in Contemporary Art*, edited by Sven Lütticken, Witte de With Center for Contemporary Art, Rotterdam, 2005, p.213.

39 Jon Ippolito, 'Introduction', in *Preserving the Immaterial: A Conference on Variable Media*, Solomon R. Guggenheim Museum, New York, 30–31 March 2001, https://www.variablemedia.net/e/preserving/html/var_pre_index .html, accessed 12 May 2020.

40 Robert Morris, in 'Session on Performative Artworks', in *Preserving the Immaterial*, op.cit.

41 Recording of *(Re)presenting Performance* symposium, 8–9 April 2005, part 2 of 2, Performances and Public Programs collection, A0068, Solomon R. Guggenheim Museum Archives, New York.

42 Amelia Jones, '"Presence" in Absentia: Experiencing Performance as Documentation', *Art Journal*, vol.56, no.4, Winter 1997, pp 11–18.

43 Recording of *(Re)presenting Performance*, op.cit.

44 See http://pastexhibitions.guggenheim.org/abramovic/, accessed 29 January 2024.

45 'Marina Abramović Interviewed', in *Seven Easy Pieces*, op.cit., p.23.

46 Barbara Clausen, 'Parallel Times Whether One's Own or That of Others: On Curating Performance Art', in *Timing: On the Temporal Dimension of Exhibiting*, edited by Beatrice von Bismarck, Rike Frank, Benjamin Meyer-Krahmer, Jörn Schafaff and Thomas Weski, Sternberg Press, Berlin, 2014, p.176.

47 Philip Auslander, 'The Performativity of Performance Documentation', *PAJ: A Journal of Performance and Art*, vol.28, no.3, September 2006, p.5.

48 Jones, '"Presence" in Absentia', op.cit., p.11.

49 Sven Lütticken, 'Performing Time', *Art Journal*, vol.70, no.3, Fall 2011, p.41.

50 Andrea Tarsia, 'Like Black Holes in a Bright White Space', *A Short History of Performance Part IV*, Whitechapel Gallery, London, 2006, p.19.

51 Valerie Casey, 'Staging Meaning: Performance in the Modern Museum', *TDR: The Drama Review*, vol.49, no.3, Autumn 2005, p.84.

52 Barbara Clausen, 'Performing the Archive and Exhibiting the Ephemeral', in *Histories of Performance Documentation*, op.cit., p.105.

53 Allan Kaprow, manuscript notes for *Baggage*, reproduced in *Allan Kaprow: Art as Life*, op.cit., p.226.

CHAPTER 3

1 Zdenka Badovinac, 'Body and the East', in *Comradeship: Curating, Art, and Politics in Post-Socialist Europe*, Independent Curators International, New York, 2019, p.57.

2   Stephanie Rosenthal (ed.), *Ana Mendieta: Traces*, Hayward Gallery, London, 2013, p.40.

3   Jones, '"Presence" in Absentia', op.cit., p.16.

4   Auslander, 'The Performativity of Performance Documentation', op.cit., p.3.

5   Sylvia Ruttimann and Karin Seinsoth, 'Interview with René Block', *On Curating*, no.22, April 2014, http://www.on-curating.org/issue -22-43/interview-with-rene-block.html#.XZHoaudKjkI, accessed 30 September 2019.

6   Sean Kelly, quoted in Julie Baumgardner, 'How Performance Art Entered the Mainstream', *Artsy*, 3 November 2015, https://www.artsy.net/article /artsy-editorial-how-performance-art-entered-the-mainstream, accessed 17 June 2020.

7   RoseLee Goldberg, 'Collecting', in *In Terms of Performance*, The Pew Center for Arts & Heritage, Philadelphia Arts Research Center, University of California, Berkeley, 2016, http://intermsofperformance.site/keywords /collecting/roselee-goldberg, accessed 8 May 2020.

8   Oral history interview with Julie B. Martin, 7–8 November 2018, Archives of American Art, Smithsonian Institution, https://www.aaa.si .edu/download_pdf_transcript/ajax?record_id=edanmdm-AAADCD _oh_397104, accessed 5 May 2020.

9   Ted Loos, 'Art-Scenes Glimpses, Lost then Found', *The New York Times*, 19 December 2013, Arts pages, p.6.

10 Christiane Berndes, in 'Van Abbemuseum, Eindhoven: Christiane Berndes, Curator and Head of Collection; and Annie Fletcher, Chief Curator', in *Histories of Performance Documentation*, op.cit., p.42.

11 See Christophe Cherix, 'Breaking Down Categories: Print Rooms, Drawing Departments, and the Museum', in *Collecting the New: Museums and Contemporary Art*, edited by Bruce Altshuler, Princeton University Press, Princeton, 2005, pp 56–8.

12 Jonah Westerman, 'Vito Acconci, Sonnabend Show Jan 72: Archives 1972', in *Performance at Tate: Into the Space of Art*, Tate Research Publication, 2016, https://www.tate.org.uk/research/publications/performance-at-tate /perspectives/vito-acconci, accessed 8 May 2020.

13 Adrian Piper, 'Notes on the Mythic Being I–III' (1974–6), in *A History of the Western Art Market. A Sourcebook of Writings on Artists, Dealers, and Markets*, edited by Titia Hulst, University of California Press, Oakland, 2017, p.95.

14 ibid., pp 95–6.

15 Claire Bishop, 'Delegated Performance: Outsourcing Authenticity', *October*, vol.140, Spring 2012, p.91.

16 Esther Ferrer, Laurence Rassel and Mar Villaespesa, 'All Variations Are Valid, Including this One', in *Esther Ferrer: All Variations Are Valid, Including this One*, Museo Nacional Centro de Arte Reina Sofía, Madrid, 2017, p.58.

17 Artist questionnaire, acquisition file for Jennifer Allora and Guillermo Calzadilla's *Stop, Repair, Prepare: Variations on Ode to Joy for a Prepared Piano, No.1*, Media and Performance, The Museum of Modern Art Archives, New York.

18 Acquisition file for Roman Ondak's *Good Feelings in Good Times*, Tate Archives, London.

19 Tania Bruguera, 'Notes on Political Specificity', *Artforum*, vol.57, no.9, May 2019, p.205.

20 Acquisition file for Tania Bruguera's *Tatlin's Whisper #5*, Tate Archives, London.

21 Acquisition file for Tania Bruguera's *Untitled (Havana, 2000)*, Media and Performance, The Museum of Modern Art Archives, New York.

22 Nelson Goodman, *Languages of Art: An Approach to a Theory of Symbols*, Bobbs-Merrill, Indianapolis, 1976, p.114.

23 *Marina Abramović Ulay / Ulay Marina Abramović 30 November / 30 November*, Harlekin Art, Wiesbaden, 1979, n.p.

24 Marc Camille Chaimovicz, press release of the exhibition *Marc Camille Chaimovicz 'Partial Eclipse'*, De Appel, Amsterdam, 1980.

25 Kateřina Šedá, *Nic tam není: společenská hra pro neomezený počet hráčů*, Brno, 2005, n.p.

26 Elizabeth Carpenter, 'Introduction', in *Living Collections Catalogue. Volume 1: On Performativity*, Walker Art Center, Minneapolis, 2014, http://walkerart .org/collections/publications/performativity/introduction, accessed 6 September 2023.

27 'Museum of Modern Art, New York: Stuart Comer, Chief Curator in the Department of Media and Performance Art; Michelle Elligott, Chief of Archives; and Ana Janevski, Associate Curator in the Department of Media and Performance Art in Conversation with Jonah Westerman, April 2015', in *Histories of Performance Documentation*, op.cit., p.17.

28 Amélie Giguère, 'Collectionner la performance: un dialogue entre l'artiste et le musée', *Muséologies*, vol.7, no.1, 2014, p.177, https://doi.org/10.7202 /1026653ar, accessed 25 June 2020 (author's translation).

29 Paul Duncan, 'Public Collection', interview with Manuel Pelmuş and Alexandra Pirici, *Revista – Arta*, 14 December 2014, https://revistaarta.ro /en/public-collection/, accessed 29 January 2024.

CHAPTER 4

1 Goldberg, 'Collecting', op.cit.

2 Catherine Wood, in Caroline Menezes, 'Tate Modern 2012 Programme in Retrospect: The Place for Performance. Conversation with Catherine Wood', *Studio International*, published 15 February 2013, https://www .studiointernational.com/index.php/tate-modern-2012-programme -in-retrospect-the-place-for-performance, accessed 26 February 2024.

3 Comer, 'Museum of Modern Art, New York', op.cit., pp 18-19.

4 Sanders, in 'Whitney Museum of American Art, New York', op.cit., p.27.

5 Mary Oliver, 'Lies, Lies, It's All Lies I Tell You!', in *Performativity in the Gallery: Staging Interactive Encounters*, edited by Outi Remes, Laura MacCulloch and Marika Leino, Peter Lang, Bern, 2014, p.17.

6 Hal Foster, *Bad New Days: Art, Criticism, Emergency*, Verso, London and New York, 2015, p.128.

7   Pablo Bronstein, 'Pablo Bronstein on How Catherine Wood Changed the Way We See Performance Art', *Frieze*, no.206, October 2019, p.139.

8   Jonah Westerman, 'Project Overview', in *Performance at Tate*, op.cit., https://www.tate.org.uk/research/publications/performance-at-tate/project-overview, accessed 20 March 2024.

9   Dominic Johnson, *Unlimited Action: The Performance of Extremity in the 1970s*, Manchester University Press, Manchester, 2019, p.4.

10 Elizabeth Armstrong, 'Fluxus and the Museum', in *In the Spirit of Fluxus*, op.cit., p.16.

11 Andreas Huyssen, 'Back to the Future: Fluxus in Context', in *In the Spirit of Fluxus*, op.cit., p.150.

12 Hannah B Higgins, 'Dead Mannequin Walking: Fluxus and the Politics of Reception', in *Perform, Repeat, Record: Live Art in History*, Intellect Books, Bristol, 2012, p.65.

13 Nancy Princenthal et al., 'Back for One Night Only!', *Art in America*, vol.94, no.2, February 2006, p.91.

14 Melanie Gilligan, 'The Beggar's Pantomime', *Artforum International*, vol.45, no.10, Summer 2007, p.428.

15 Amelia Jones, 'The Artist is Present: Artistic Re-enactments and the Impossibility of "Presence"', *TDR: The Drama Review*, vol.55, no.1, Spring 2011, p.19.

16 Rosenthal, 'Agency for Action', op.cit., p.57.

17 André Lepecki, 'Redoing 18 Happenings in 6 Parts', in *Allan Kaprow: 18 Happenings in 6 Parts*, Steidl, Göttingen, 2007, p.48.

18 ibid.

19 Sabine Breitwieser, 'Taking Part in the Museum', *Afterall: A Journal of Art, Context and Enquiry*, no.34, Autumn / Winter 2013, p.9.

20 Bishop, 'Delegated Performance', op.cit., p.105.

21 'In Conversation with Lois Keidan', in *Live Forever. Collecting Live Art*, edited by Teresa Calonje, Koenig, London, 2014, pp 73–4.

22 Claire Bishop, 'The Perils and Possibilities of Dance in the Museum: Tate, MoMA, and Whitney', *Dance Research Journal*, vol.46, no.3, Special Issue: Dance in the Museum, December 2014, p.54.

23 Gilligan, 'The Beggar's Pantomime', op.cit., p.429.

24 Catherine Wood, *Performance in Contemporary Art*, Tate Publishing, London, 2018, p.23.

25 Bronstein, 'Pablo Bronstein on How Catherine Wood Changed the Way We See Performance Art', op.cit., p.139.

26 Catherine Wood, in *Agency: A Partial History of Live Art*, edited by Theron Schmidt, Intellect, Bristol, Chicago and London / Live Art Development Agency, 2019, p.147.

27 Mark Franko and André Lepecki, 'Editors' Note: Dance in the Museum', *Dance Research Journal*, vol.46, no.3, December 2014, p.1.

28 Claire Bishop, *Disordered Attention: How We Look at Art and Performance Today*, Verso, London and New York, 2024, p.80.

29 ibid.

30 Boris Charmatz, 'Manifesto for the Dancing Museum', 2009, https://www.moma.org/ momaorg/shared/pdfs/docs/calendar/manifesto_dancing_museum.pdf, accessed 15 April 2024.

31 *Infinite Experience*, Museo de Arte Latinoamericano de Buenos Aires website, https://www.malba.org.ar/en/evento/experiencia-infinita/, accessed 11 March 2024.

32 Kathy Halbreich, 'Foreword', in *In the Spirit of Fluxus*, op.cit., p.11.

33 Sanders, 'Whitney Museum of American Art, New York', op.cit., p.22.

34 Elizabeth Carpenter, 'Introduction', in *Living Collections Catalogue. Volume 1: On Performativity*, Walker Art Center, Minneapolis, 2014, https://walkerart .org/collections/publications/performativity/introduction/, accessed 4 April 2024.

35 ibid.

36 Pip Laurenson, 'Charisma and Desire in the Conservation of Performance Art', in *Performance: The Ethics and the Politics of Conservation and Care, Volume 1*, edited by Hanna B. Hölling, Jules Pelta Feldman and Emilie Magnin, Routledge, London and New York, 2023, p.36.

37 'The Live List: What to Consider When Collecting Live Works', Collecting the Performative Network, 24 January 2014, https://www.tate.org.uk /about-us/projects/collecting-performative/live-list-what-consider-when -collecting-live-works, accessed 4 April 2024.

38 ibid.

39 Susannah Schouweiler, 'Collecting Performance', 2011, https://walkerart .org/magazine/collecting-performance, accessed 4 April 2024.

40 ibid.

41 Louise Lawson, Acatia Finbow and Hélia Marçal, 'Developing a Strategy for the Conservation of Performance-based Artworks at Tate', *Journal of the Institute of Conservation*, vol.42, no.2, 2019, p.114.

42 Hanna B. Hölling, Jules Pelta Feldman and Emilie Magnin, 'Introduction: Caring for Performance', in *Performance: The Ethics and the Politics of Conservation and Care, Volume 1*, op.cit., p.1.

43 Dorothea von Hantelmann, *How to Do Things with Art: The Meaning of Art's Performativity*, JRP Ringier, Zürich, and Les Presses du Réel, Dijon, 2010, p.134.

44 Vivian van Saaze, 'In the Absence of Documentation: Remembering Tino Sehgal's Constructed Situations', in *Performing Documentation in the Conservation of Contemporary Art*, edited by Gunnar Heydenreich, Rita Macedo and Lúcia Matos, Instituto de História da Arte, Lisbon, 2015, p.61.

45 Athena Christa Holbrook, 'Second-Generation Huddle. A Communal Approach to Collecting and Conserving Simone Forti's Dance Constructions at The Museum of Modern Art', *VDR-Beiträge zur Erhaltung von Kunst- und Kulturgut*, vol.5, no.1, 2018, p.121.

46 'Interview: Boris Charmatz and Ana Janevski', edited by Leora Morinis, Museum of Modern Art, New York, https://www.moma.org/momaorg /shared/pdfs/docs/calendar/charmatz-janevski-inteview.pdf, accessed 15 April 2024.

47 Talya Epstein on Simone Forti Workshops, Danspace Project, 2017, https://danspaceproject.org/2017/02/07/talya-epstein-on-simone-forti -workshops/, accessed 18 February 2024.

48 Holbrook, 'Second-Generation Huddle', op.cit., p.122.

1   Nat Trotman, quoted in Deborah Vankin, 'Can Performance Art Be Owned?
    Why the Genre is Often Missing in Museum Collections', *Los Angeles Times*,
    8 August 2019, https://www.latimes.com/entertainment-arts/story/2019
    -08-07/moca-xu-zhen-performance-art, accessed 5 May 2020.
2   Bishop, 'Delegated Performance', op.cit., p.102.
3   Sabine Breitwieser, 'From the Modern to the Global Museum: Collecting
    Interdisciplinary and Non-Object-Based Art', Interdisciplinary Initiative
    at the Walker, 2016–2020, Walker Art Center, Minneapolis, 5 November
    2019, https://walkerart.org/magazine/from-the-modern-to-the-global
    -museum-collecting-interdisciplinary-and-non-object-based-art#_ftn6,
    accessed 22 January 2024.
4   ibid.
5   Philip Bither, 'Collecting', in *In Terms of Performance*, op.cit.,
    http://intermsofperformance.site/keywords/collecting/philip-bither,
    accessed 8 May 2020.
6   Breitwieser, 'From the Modern to the Global Museum', op.cit.

Further Reading

Bishop, Claire, *Disordered Attention: How We Look at Art and Performance Today*.
    London, New York: Verso, 2024.
Calonje, Teresa (ed.), *Live Forever. Collecting Live Art*. London: Koenig, 2014.
Giannachi, Gabriella, and Jonah Westerman (eds), *Histories of Performance
    Documentation: Museum, Artistic, and Scholarly Practices*. London, New York:
    Routledge, 2018.
Hölling, Hanna B., Jules Pelta Feldman and Emilie Magnin (eds), *Performance:
    The Ethics and the Politics of Conservation and Care, Volume 1*. London,
    New York: Routledge, 2023.
Muñoz-Viñas, Salvador, *Contemporary Theory of Conservation*. London:
    Routledge, 2015.
Remes, Outi, Laura MacCulloch and Marika Leino (eds), *Performativity
    in the Gallery: Staging Interactive Encounters*. Bern: Peter Lang, 2014.
Tate Research Publication, *Performance at Tate: Into the Space of Art*, 2016.
    https://www.tate.org.uk/research/publications/performance-at-tate.
von Bismarck, Beatrice, Rike Frank, Benjamin Meyer-Krahmer, Jörn Schafaff
    and Thomas Weski, *Timing: On the Temporal Dimension of Exhibiting*. Berlin:
    Sternberg Press, 2014.

Index

Image Credits

1 Marta Minujín Archive; 2 Paul Brandenburg / mkp.ZERO.1.V.202, ZERO foundation, Düsseldorf; 3 Digital image, The Museum of Modern Art, New York / Scala, Florence; 4 Projeto Hélio Oiticica & Desdémone Bardin; 5 Courtesy Oscar Bony Estate; 6 Harald Szeemann papers, Getty Research Institute, Los Angeles (2011.M.30) © Estate of Wolf Vostell / Artists Rights Society (ARS), New York / VG Bild-Kunst, Bonn. © DACS 2024; 7 © Chris Burden / licensed by The Chris Burden Estate and DACS 2020; 8 Museum of Contemporary Art Chicago / Art Resource, NY; 9 Collection Walker Art Center, Minneapolis; T.B. Walker Acquisition Fund, with additional funds from Lila and Gilbert Silverman, 1993; 10 © Centre Pompidou, MNAM-CCI Bibliothèque Kandinsky, Dist. RMN-Grand Palais / Jean-Claude Planchet; 11 Whitechapel Gallery, Whitechapel Gallery Archive. © 2025 Carolee Schneemann Foundation / your society. Courtesy Lisson Gallery and P·P·O·W, New York. 2025; 12 Marina Abramović Archives; 13 Barbara Visser; 14 Acquired with funding from Museumsfonden af 7. December 1966; Photograph courtesy of Louisiana Museum of Modern Art; 15 Macba / Barcelona © Adagp; 16 Tate; 17 The Museum of Modern Art Archives, New York © Photo SCALA, Florence. © Vito Acconci / Artists Rights Society (ARS), New York, courtesy Maria Acconci 2024; 18 Generali Foundation Collection-Permanent Loan to the Museum der Moderne Salzburg, © Generali Foundation, photo: (see Schedule / .1) © DACS 2023; photograph by Werner Kaligofsky; 19 Van Abbemuseum, Eindhoven, The Netherlands; 20 Digital image, The Museum of Modern Art, New York / Scala, Florence. Photograph by Jonathan Muzikar.

Acknowledgements

The idea of this book originates from research I undertook for a new
a new lecture at Sotheby's Institute of Art in London, and I would like
to thank students for the joy of working with them.

I am profoundly grateful to Marcus Verhagen for believing in this
project from the start and making it possible. I have gained enormously
from his guidance and from the invaluable editorial assistance of Lucy
Myers at Lund Humphries at important stages of the writing process.
I am also indebted to Sylvie Coëllier and Anna Moszynska for their sound
comments, advice and suggestions. At Sotheby's Institute, I have greatly
benefited from generous funding, from the help of the librarians and
from the support of Juliet Hacking.

Academics, archivists, artists, curators, librarians, registrars and
other people have helped make this book happen by exchanging ideas,
sharing information and facilitating access to documents. I especially
wish to thank Zdenka Badovinac, Fabio Balducci, Marie Cool, Paul
Galloway, Fanny Gonella, Athena Christa Holbrook, Martha Joseph,
Kate Scherer and Katy Wan, who generously gave of their time for
discussions. For their kind assistance, I would also like to thank
Beate Bischoff, Behiye Bobaroğlu, Jean-Philippe Bonilli, Lyn Calzia,
Jean Charlier, Lisa Cole, Louise Nicole Cone, Harriet Curtis, Cristina
D'Alessandro, Meike Deilmann, Camille Delattre, Matthew Gengler,
Kim Hansen, Kelly Kivland, Doris Krystof, Suzanne Lacy, Louise
Lawson, Sook-Kyung Lee, Doris Leutgeb, Fernanda Lopes, Cátia
Louredo, Ilan Michel, Liana Radvak, Robert Whitman and Mada
Zielińska, and the artists who have given permission to reproduce
their work.

I wish to thank my partner for his unwavering patience during
the writing of this book.